W9-ATF-794

2nd
edition

Using SPSS
for Social Statistics *and*
Research Methods

For my sister, Becky, my brother, Ben, and in loving memory of our Grandmom Betty . . .

2nd
edition

Using SPSS
for Social Statistics *and*
Research Methods

William E. Wagner, III

California State University, Channel Islands

PINE FORGE PRESS
An Imprint of SAGE Publications, Inc.
Los Angeles • London • New Delhi • Singapore • Washington DC

For information:

Pine Forge Press
An Imprint of SAGE
   Publications, Inc.
2455 Teller Road
Thousand Oaks, California 91320
E-mail: order@sagepub.com

SAGE Publications Ltd.
1 Oliver's Yard
55 City Road
London, EC1Y 1SP
United Kingdom

SAGE Publications India Pvt. Ltd.
B 1/I 1 Mohan Cooperative
   Industrial Area
Mathura Road, New Delhi 110 044
India

SAGE Publications
   Asia-Pacific Pte. Ltd.
33 Pekin Street #02-01
Far East Square
Singapore 048763

Printed in the United States of America

Library of Congress Cataloging-in-Publication Data

Wagner, William E. (William Edward)
Using SPSS for social statistics and research methods : / William E. Wagner, III. — 2nd ed.
    p. cm.
ISBN 978-1-4129-7333-5 (pbk.)
    1. Social sciences—Statistical methods. 2. SPSS for Windows. I. Title.

HA32.W34 2009
300.285′555—dc22   2008050868

This book is printed on acid-free paper.

09   10   11   12   13   10   9   8   7   6   5   4   3   2

Acquisitions Editor:	Jerry Westby
Editorial Assistant:	Eve Oettinger
Production Editor:	Brittany Bauhaus
Copy Editor:	Gillian Dickens
Typesetter:	C&M Digitals (P) Ltd.
Proofreader:	Sally Jaskold
Cover Designer:	Glenn Vogel
Marketing Manager:	Jennifer Reed Banando

Contents

Preface

This book was written for those learning introductory statistics or with some basic statistics knowledge who want to use SPSS Statistics software to manage data and/or carry out basic statistical analyses. It can also be a useful tool to gain an understanding of how SPSS Statistics software works before going on to more complicated statistical procedures. This volume is an ideal supplement for a statistics or research methods course. While it can be used with any research methods or statistics book or materials, it was tailored to complement *Investigating the Social World,* by Russell Schutt (2009), and *Social Statistics for a Diverse Society,* by Chava Frankfort-Nachmias and Anna Leon-Guerrero (2009). It can also be used as a guide for those working with basic statistics on their own. The book provides information for users about some of the important mechanics of SPSS Statistics operating procedures for simple data management along with accessible introductory statistical instructions.

References

Frankfort-Nachmias, C., & Leon-Guerrero, A. (2009). *Social statistics for a diverse society* (5th ed.). Thousand Oaks, CA: Pine Forge Press.

Schutt, R. (2009). *Investigating the social world* (6th ed.). Thousand Oaks, CA: Pine Forge Press.

Acknowledgments

M any thanks go to Jerry Westby at Sage/Pine Forge Press for his support and vision. Anna Leon-Guerrero and Russell Schutt were particularly helpful, providing insightful reviews and productive suggestions.

The author and SAGE gratefully acknowledge the contributions of the following reviewers:

J. Joy Esquierdo, *University of Texas Pan American*

P. Rafael Hernández-Arias, *DePaul University*

James Kiwanuka-Tondo, *North Carolina State University*

Carol Silverman, *University of San Francisco*

Scott Vollum, *James Madison University*

David Wilson, *University of Delaware*

1

Overview

This book will serve as a guide for those interested in using SPSS Statistics software to aid in statistical data analysis—whether as a companion to a statistics or research methods course or whether as a stand-alone guide for a particular project or individual learning. The images and directions used in this book come from SPSS Statistics Version 17.0, released in the fall of 2008. This manual can be used to supplement a statistics or research methods class and/or textbook, although it can also be used as a guide by itself to aid in the process of data analysis using the SPSS software.

Statistical Software

The SPSS software works with several kinds of computer files: data files, output files, and syntax files. Data files are those computer files that contain the information that the user intends to analyze. Output files contain the statistical analysis and often tables, graphs, and/or charts. Syntax files are computer instructions that tell the SPSS software what to do. Syntax files are not used in the student version of the SPSS software and are dealt with as an advanced application in Chapter 11 of this book.

The General Social Survey (GSS) serves the secondary data set used as an example to demonstrate typical functions of the program. While SPSS is the software program, produced by SPSS, Inc., of Chicago, Illinois, the GSS is a data set that is read and analyzed by the SPSS software; it is a data file containing the information to be analyzed. The two things are distinct and can be used in separate contexts without the other.

About the General Social Survey Data

The National Opinion Research Center (NORC) at the University of Chicago administers the GSS. The GSS was started in 1972 and continues to the present time. The data used for the examples in this book come from the latest available completed version of the GSS, from 2006. According to NORC, with the exception of the U.S. census, the GSS is the most frequently analyzed source of information in the social sciences. According to NORC, there are at least 14,000 instances when the GSS has been used for articles in scholarly journals, books, and doctoral dissertations. Furthermore, it is estimated that more than 400,000 students annually use the GSS in their work.

The GSS contains many demographic and attitudinal questions, as well as rotating topics of special interest. A number of core questions have remained unchanged in each survey since 1972. This allows for rich longitudinal research about the attitudes, opinions, and demographics in the United States. Topical questions appear sometimes for just one year; other times, they can appear for a period of years. Therefore, the GSS is versatile as a longitudinal data resource and a relevant cross-sectional resource.

SPSS Electronic Files

SPSS Statistics 17.0 uses different file extensions, or *endings,* and associated icons to signify types of files. For instance, a file named "file.sav" is a data file called "file." The ".sav" is used to signify that this is a data file. Again, data files contain the information that SPSS is used to analyze. A file with the extension ".sps" is an SPSS Statistics syntax file, while a file with the extension ".spv" (or ".spo" for older versions of SPSS software) is an SPSS Statistics output file. Output files contain SPSS analysis and such things as charts, tables, and other information. Syntax files contain coded instructions for SPSS to perform operations on data and to produce output. It is not necessary to create, save, or even deal with syntax files for most basic SPSS functions; therefore, syntax files will be covered only to the level of description and simple use in Chapter 11.

Opening Existing Data Files

To open an SPSS data file that you already have or have obtained, select the "File" menu, then choose "Open" and select "Data." (For other file types, see the section on importing data from non-SPSS file formats.) At this point, you will need to navigate the disk drives (or network drives or other sorts of storage devices) to locate the data file that you wish to open. Once you locate the file, either double-click it or click it once and click the "Open" button toward the bottom right side of the "Open File" dialog box.

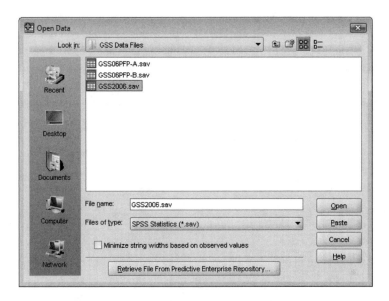

SPSS will then open the data file, and you will be presented with the information in a grid format (somewhat similar to a Microsoft Excel environment). You have choices about both the way the information is presented and the information you see. For example, you can choose to see the "Data View," presented in the following image. Note that the variables are listed in columns, with each case recorded as a row. The variable "age" has been selected as a reference point. The data in that column tell the ages of each respondent.

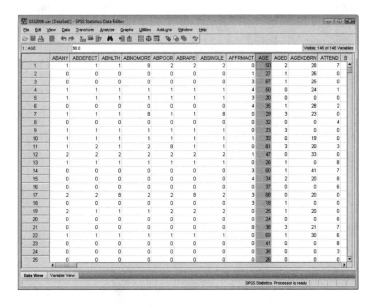

Now, click on the "Variable View" tab, which is located toward the bottom left of the screen. Note that the "Data View" tab is currently selected and is the default when opening a new file with SPSS 17. While the information looks somewhat different, you are still looking at the same data file. See the following image.

Again, the "age" variable has been selected for reference. In this view, variables are depicted in rows, with information about the variables, such as variable label, category labels, type, level of measurement, and so on. You can add to, edit, or delete any of the variable information contained in this view by directly typing into the cells. This view does not show the actual response data; to view that, you would need to select the "Data View" option.

Importing Data From Non-SPSS File Formats

There is often a need to analyze existing data files that were not created or formatted by SPSS software. These files might be created by other statistical software packages (e.g., SAS or STATA) or by other types of numeric programs (e.g., Microsoft Excel). To open these files, first select the same menu options you would as if you were opening an SPSS data file:

FILE → OPEN → DATA

Now, at the "Files of type" prompt at the bottom of the dialog box, click the arrow at the right to expand the choices. Next, select "Excel (*.xls, *.xlsx, *.xlsm)." You will need to navigate your hard drive, other drives, or locations to find your file. Once you locate the file, select and open it. At this point, you will be presented with a new dialog box.

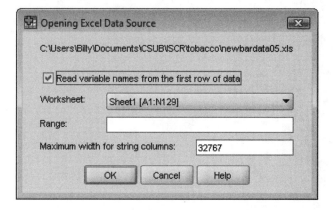

If the column headings in the Microsoft Excel file contain the variable names, then make sure the box asking to "Read variable names from the first row of data" is selected. If the column headings are not formatted in a way that conforms to the SPSS variable-naming conventions, then they will be transformed into permitted variable names, and the original names will be recorded as variable labels.

To import only a portion of the Excel file, enter the range of cells from which you would like to import data.

It is also possible to import files from databases, text files, and other sources. Follow the same instructions as with Excel files, except for the file type you select. Depending on the file type you choose, you will be presented with different dialog boxes or wizards to import the data.

In some cases, you may simply have unlabeled data in a particular file, or the variable names or other information may be of little or no use to you. In that case, depending on the size of the file, you could copy the data from the original numeric program (e.g., Microsoft Excel) and then paste it directly into the SPSS "Data View" window. This is particularly useful if you just want to add numeric values from another source and enter or program the other information using SPSS.

Opening Previously Created Output Files

To open a previously created output file, select from the "File" menu as follows.

FILE → OPEN → OUTPUT

You will be presented with the following dialog box:

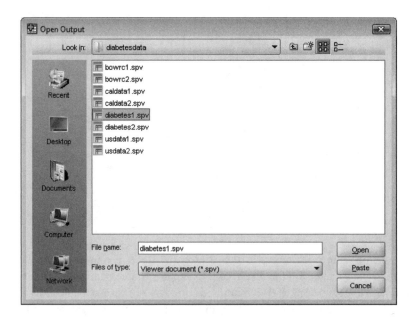

Here, just navigate to find your file, as you would any other type of file. Once you locate it, select and open the file. SPSS will open the file into an "Output Viewer" window. There, you can view and edit it. Note that Version 17 (as well as Version 16) of SPSS Statistics uses the *.spv file extension, as opposed to the *.spo file extension used in prior versions of this software. SPSS 17 is capable of opening output files created with older versions of SPSS.

Saving Files

Saving any type of SPSS file is performed in virtually the same way as with any modern computer program. Select either

FILE → SAVE   To save the file as the currently assigned name

or

FILE → SAVE AS   To save the file in a different file, under a new name

The first option, will automatically save the file without prompting you for a dialog box, unless you are working with a new, yet unnamed, file. In that case, you will get the same type of dialog box as though you had selected the "Save As" option. If you do choose the second option, you will be given a dialog box prompting you to name the file and to select the location on your computer or network where the file is to be placed.

Creating New SPSS Data Files

To create a new SPSS data file, select the "File" menu, then choose "New" and select "Data."

FILE → NEW → DATA

You will be given a blank "Data Editor" window. You can immediately start entering information about the variables you wish to create and/or the actual data codes that you may have. In the "Data Editor" window that follows, information has been entered for two variables: age and sex. The "Variable View" tab has been selected. Notice that the labels have been entered, and other information about the variables has been selected.

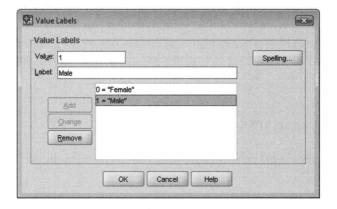

For the sex variable, value labels have been entered. This was done by clicking on the "Values" cell for that variable and then selecting the button with three small dots. The following dialog box would have appeared:

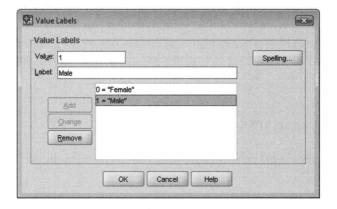

In the "Value Labels" box, you can enter the label for each of the category codes for the variable. In this case, "0" was entered in the "Value" box, while "Female" was entered into the "Label" box. At that point, to record the information, you must click the "Add" button. Notice, also, that "1" was entered into the "Value" box, "Male" was entered into the "Label" box, and again, the "Add" button was clicked. (This procedure also produces a dummy variable called "male," where the value of 1 is male, and 0 is "not male.")

It is also possible to enter the data directly into the "Data Editor." To do this, click the "Data View" tab at the lower left of the "Data Editor" window. The columns now represent the newly created variables: age and sex.

Creating and Editing SPSS Output Files

Output files are created by SPSS when you instruct the software to perform functions. For example, if you request SPSS to provide frequencies and central tendency values for three variables from your data set, then an output file will automatically be produced (unless one is already open), and the information that you have requested will be presented in the "Output Viewer" window. To edit the output, you'll select and double-click the part you wish to work with, and there are tools to facilitate that task. More information on this topic will be provided in Chapter 4: Organization and Presentation of Information.

Preferences: Getting Started

To change the settings, parameters, and preferences for the SPSS program, select the edit menu and choose "Options."

EDIT → OPTIONS

You will be given a dialog box like the one shown here:

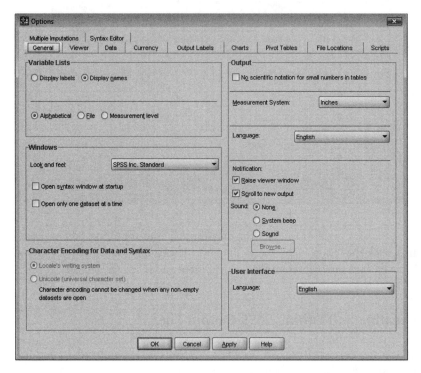

Numerous features can be controlled using this dialog box, and most are intuitive in their operation. As a user becomes more experienced, she or he often uses more of these features. From the start, however, most SPSS users will want to make sure that variables will be displayed throughout the program in alphabetical order and also by name (rather than label). This can be done by selecting the "General" tab and clicking the radio buttons for "Display names" and "Alphabetical."

This is particularly important if you are using or creating a data set that contains a large number of variables, such as the GSS. While it is clear that alphabetizing the list will facilitate easier access to variables, listing by name is also crucial since variable labels are more detailed and may not necessarily begin with or even use the same letters as the variable name. Changing or verifying these settings upfront can save a good deal of time and frustration. If a data set is opened and the preferences have not been set to the desired parameters, the user can still go to the dialog box and make the change while the data set is open. (In some older versions of SPSS, it would be necessary to close the data set, make the change, and reopen data set.)

To get a quick overview of the variables in a given data set, you can access a variable utility window in SPSS that provides useful information about each of the variables in a way that can be easily navigated (and such that information can be easily pasted to output if desired). By opening this window, the importance of organized naming and ordering of variables in a large data file can be exemplified. Choose the "Utilities" menu, then select "Variables."

UTILITIES → VARIABLES

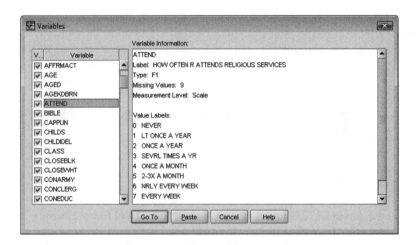

When selecting a variable from the alphabetized list of variable names on the left, information about that particular variable will appear on the right side of the box, including the label, the level of measurement, and the value labels. This is a fast way to determine what kind of variables are available in your data set that are suited to different statistical methods of analysis.

Measurement of Variables Using SPSS

Whether creating a new data file with SPSS or using an existing data file, it is important to understand how variables have been measured, or "treated," by the creator of the data file. This "treatment" is a factor of how the data were collected—how much information is contained within the data set about a variable.

First, it is important to be aware that SPSS can record variables as either *string* variables or *numeric* variables. String variables can consist of letters and/or numbers and cannot be treated numerically; therefore, string variables must be treated at the nominal level of measurement. Numeric variables use numbers to represent response values. These numbers may represent actual numbers, ranked categories, or unranked categories. In other words, numeric variables may be nominal, ordinal, interval, or ratio.

In social science statistics and research methods courses, variables are typically described as nominal, ordinal, interval, or ratio. Many textbooks, such as *Investigating the Social World*, by Russell Schutt (2009), elaborate all four of those categories. In some texts, interval and ratio measures are combined, as is the case in *Social Statistics for a Diverse Society*, by Chava Frankfort-Nachmias and Anna Leon-Guerrero (2009).

SPSS Statistics uses these codes for levels of measurement: nominal, ordinal, and scale. *Nominal* and *ordinal* both correspond to the concepts with the same names. The *scale* denotation corresponds with interval-ratio, interval, and ratio. There are functions within the SPSS software that will limit your ability to conduct analyses or create graphs based on the recognized level of measurement. Therefore, it is important to verify that the indicator in the "Measurement" column of the variable view is correct for all variables you will use in your analyses.

References

Frankfort-Nachmias, C., & Leon-Guerrero, A. (2009). *Social statistics for a diverse society* (5th ed.). Thousand Oaks, CA: Pine Forge Press.

Schutt, R. (2009). *Investigating the social world* (6th ed.). Thousand Oaks, CA: Pine Forge Press.

2

Transforming Variables

In this chapter, tools for restructuring variables will be introduced. SPSS allows for numerous ways to reconfigure, combine, and compute variable data.

Recoding and Computing Variables

Often, one must reorganize the way data are recorded before performing statistical analyses. This might be due to the level of measurement of a particular variable that a researcher wishes to change, or it could be related to the researcher's intended use of a variable. One may wish to collapse a few categories of a variable into one for appropriateness of analysis. For example, within the marital status variable, one might combine "married" and "separated" categories to form "legally married," as well as combine "divorced" along with "single never married" to form "unmarried." "Recoding" is the SPSS function that allows the researcher to recategorize the variable to suit the needs of the analysis.

There are many times when a researcher needs to produce a new variable from existing information in a data set, but that information is not contained solely within one variable. SPSS has a "Compute" function that allows a user to both perform mathematical operations on variable data and combine data from multiple distinct variables within the file.

Recoding Variables

For this recoding example, we will use the General Social Survey (GSS) 2006 data set. We will take a straightforward case of dichotomizing age from a ratio variable, presenting the respondent's actual age at the time of interview, into just two categories with a cut point of 50 years of age. To recode or change the categories of a variable, select the "Transform" menu, then choose the "Recode" option, and then select "Into Different Variables."

TRANSFORM→ RECODE → INTO DIFFERENT VARIABLES

You will then be given a dialog box like the one displayed here:

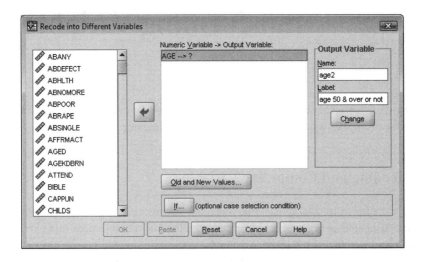

It is useful and proactive against data loss to recode into "different variables" rather than "same variables" if you are reducing information contained within the variable. For instance, if you are recoding a ratio-level variable into an ordinal or a dichotomous variable, then you would want to create a different variable. The reason behind this is that the lost information resulting from the recode would still be retained in the original variable should you want to change the way in which you recode the variable at some point later or if you determine that you need the more detailed ratio-level information for your current analysis.

Recoding Variables: Dichotomies and Dummy Variables

In this example, we recode the "AGE" variable into a dichotomy: a variable with exactly two categories, not including missing values. A dummy variable is a dichotomy usually coded with a value of "1" to indicate the existence of a particular attribute. All other attributes are coded "0" as an indication that the particular attribute from "1," as well as usually the name of the variable itself, is not present. Dummy variables are particularly useful for many statistical operations, including multiple regression models (see Chapter 7: Correlation and Regression Analysis). It is also possible to use a series of dummy variables to represent several attributes from a given nominal variable.

To dichotomize the age variable, first select "AGE" from the list of variables in the data set on the left, then click the arrow to move it to the "Numeric Variable" box. Now, create a new name for the variable; in this example, the mundane "age2" has been conjured. You may also select a label at this time, or you can attend to that at a later time through the "Variable View" screen. For this example, the label, "age 50 & over or not," was added. While it has not been done yet in the screen image above, the next step is to click the "Change" button. This will enter the name "age2" into the "Output Variable" location, where there is currently a "?" acting as a placeholder.

Now, it is necessary to give SPSS the instructions for *how* the variable is to be recoded. In this example, we want to change all ages up to and including 49 into a category, call it "0," and all ages 50 and older into another category, call it "1." Click on the "Old and New Values" button in the dialog box, and another dialog box will appear on top, like the one that follows:

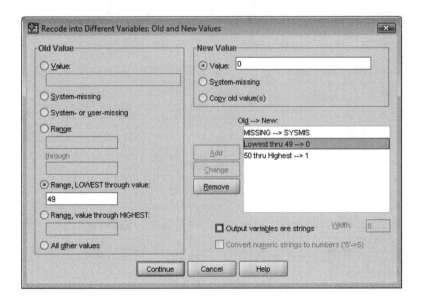

To implement the changes, first, under "Old Value," select the radio button that reads, "Range, LOWEST through value." Then enter "49" in the box underneath. Then, under "New Value," select "Value" and enter "0." Now, click the "Add" button. This instructs SPSS to transform all ages up to and including 49 into category 0.

Next, under "Old Value," select the radio button associated with "Range, value through Highest." Enter 50 in the box beneath that heading. Then, under "New Value," select "Value" and enter "1." Again, click the "Add" button. This now instructs SPSS to transform all ages 50 and beyond into category 1.

Next, under "Old Value," select "System- or user-missing." Under "New Value," select "System-missing." This will ensure that missing values continue to be treated as such, even if they had been recorded as numeric values. Click the "Add" button once again to confirm this instruction.

Now your instructions have been entered and you can click the "Continue" button; this will close the current dialog box and return you to the original "Recode into Different Variables" dialog box. Once there, you must click the "OK" button for SPSS to process your request to recode and then create the new variable.

If the "OK" is dimmed and SPSS will not allow you to click it, then one of the above steps must not have been completed. The one most often overlooked is clicking on the "Change" button, which adds the new variable name for the output variable.

Notice that the new variable is appended to the bottom of the variable list in the "Variable View" of the "Data Editor" window. You can move that variable to another place in the list if you wish by selecting it, then dragging it between two of the other variables.

Since this is a newly created variable, it is very important to insert value labels. If the variable label and/or value labels are not clear, then it can be easy to forget what the values are or in which direction the variable was coded. Click the cell in the "Values" column for the variable to which you want to append value labels. Then click the button with three dots (. . .).

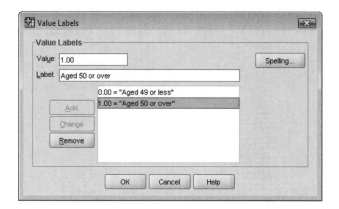

The "Value Labels" dialog box will pop up. As before with value labels, enter both the value and the label. Then click the "Add" button after each value and label that you enter. When all value/label combinations have been entered, then click "OK." The value labels will then be updated. You can inspect the value labels in the "Variable View" window of SPSS by clicking on the button with three dots on it in the "Values" column of the variable (age2).

Computing Variables

There are numerous reasons why a user of SPSS would be interested in computing a new variable. For example, one may want to construct an index from individual questions, or one may wish to compute the logarithmic (log) function of a particular variable. In this example, we want to compute the average education level of the respondents' parents. So, we will add mother's education level to father's education level and then divide by two. (In more sophisticated approaches, we might divide by the number of parental responses.)

To perform the computation, select these menus:

TRANSFORM → COMPUTE . . .

The "Compute Variable" dialog box will be presented.

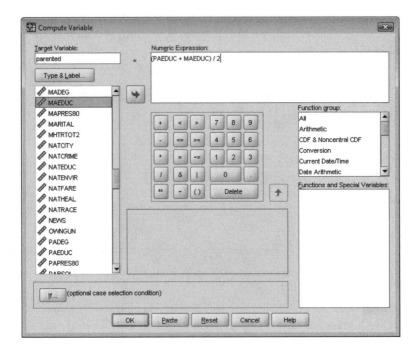

Type the name you wish to assign to the new variable in the "Target Variable" box. Next, prepare the computation equation in the "Numeric Expression" box. In this case, it is necessary to select the parentheses, ( ), first. Then, insert the "maeduc" variable, as well as an addition sign, followed by the "paeduc" variable into the parentheses. Now, put a divisor bar after the parentheses, and click the number "2." This has the effect of adding together the total years of education of both parents and then dividing by two, yielding the average.

Note the functions that are available to use. Statistical, trigonometric, date, time, and string functions, among others, can be used to compute just about anything. Also, if you wish to set up a conditional computation—such that a computation is only made in one case, or there are to be different computations for different cases, based on some predetermined condition—then select the "If" button, and enter that/those condition(s). The same functions and keypads are provided to instruct SPSS how to determine the criteria for the conditional computation.

Using the Count Function

SPSS Statistics Version 17 allows users the option to add particular values across variables. Suppose a researcher wanted to count the number of instances where a respondent gave a yes answer to particular questions. For this example, consider the GSS (2006) series of questions on opinions relating to abortion. Use the menus below to carry out this example:

TRANSFORM → COUNT VALUES WITHIN CASES . . .

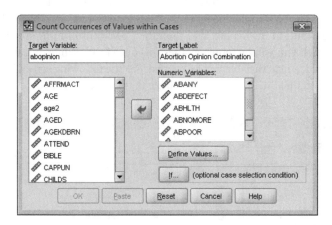

In the dialog box that appears, move the appropriate variables from the variable list on the left into the "Numeric Variables" box. It will also be necessary to enter a name for the new variable to be created in the "Target Variable" slot. The target label can be conveniently entered in the appropriate slot as well. Next, click the "Define Values" button. The following dialog box will be provided:

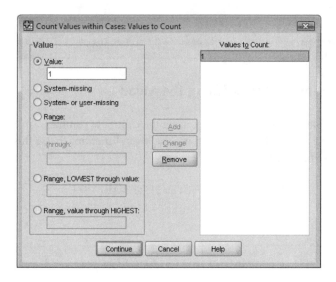

Here, you will want to select the values to be counted. For the opinion questions that have been selected in this example, a code of 1 indicates an affirmative response (while a 2 indicates a negative response). Therefore, we want to count the number of responses that have a value of 1. Click the radio button next to "Value" at the upper left of the dialog box, then enter a "1" into the associated slot beneath. Now, click the "Add" button in the middle of the dialog box. The "1" should appear in the "Values to Count" area. Now, click the "Continue" button in this box and then the "OK" button in the prior dialog box, to which you will be returned after this one closes. While output will not be generated, a new variable will be created. See the following screen image for the data contained within the new variable that has been created.

Computing an Index Using the Mean

It is possible to construct an index using the Compute command in SPSS. The most direct way of doing this is to use the Mean function. To use this method, click these menus:

TRANSFORM → COMPUTE VARIABLE . . .

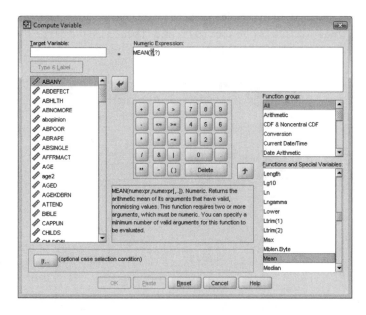

When presented with the "Compute Variable" dialog box, select "Mean" from the "Functions and Special Variables" box in the lower right corner. Make sure "Function group" is set to "All." After you select "Mean," click the up-arrow sending mean to the "Numeric Expression" area. It will appear as it does in the preceding image. You must insert all of the variables of interest within the parentheses, each separated by a comma. See the following dialog box for how this is done in the current example.

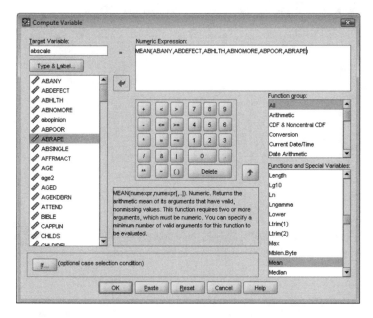

After selecting the variables from the bank on the left, enter the target variable (new variable to be created) name. Then click the "Type & Label" button. The following short dialog box will be provided:

Click the radio button next to "Label" and enter the appropriate variable label in the adjacent slot. Now, click "Continue," then "OK." A new variable, abscale, will be created and appear in the SPSS "Data Editor" window as shown below.

In this case of nonmissing data, notice that the value computed for the mean falls between (and including) 1 and 2. This is because 1 represents yes and 2 represents no. For statistical purposes, it is sometimes beneficial to have a result between 0 and 1 instead. To arrange for this, you can also subtract the number 1 from the completed mean function in the original compute box, or you can go back now and make the change, as is exhibited as follows. Again, click these menus:

TRANSFORM → COMPUTE VARIABLE . . .

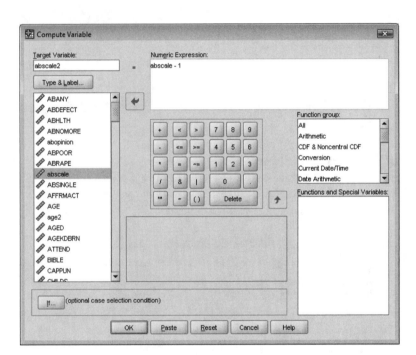

If the given dialog box is populated with data, click the "Reset" button at the bottom of the box. Now, enter a name for the new variable. (While not recommended, you could overwrite the original variable name.) In the "Numeric Expression" area, move the original variable from the bank on the left. Then, on the calculator-style keypad, click "-" and then "1." This will subtract one from each case and move the data means into the desired range, as they are in the following screen image.

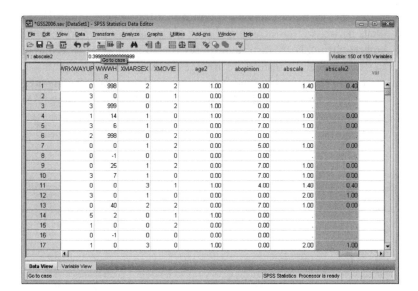

Multiple Response

To produce multiple response values (e.g., frequency values combined across multiple variables), choose the following menus:

ANALYZE → MULTIPLE RESPONSE → DEFINE SETS . . .

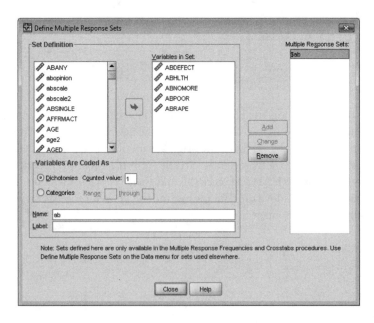

From the variable bank on the left, move all of the desired variables into the "Variables in Set" box. In this example, the variables chosen are dichotomies, and we are counting the yes value, 1. It is also possible to select a category and range. Now, name the set and type the name in the "Name" slot. You also have the opportunity to place a label at this time. Finally, click the "Add" button on the right side of the dialog box. You can now click "Close."

To produce a frequency table for the response set that has just been identified, click the following menus:

ANALYZE → MULTIPLE RESPONSE → FREQUENCIES . . .

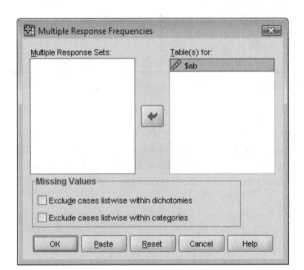

Select the response set from the list on the left (in this case, it was the only item in the list). Move the set to the "Table(s) for" box. Then, click "OK." SPSS will produce output such as the following:

Case Summary

	\multicolumn{6}{c}{Cases}					
	\multicolumn{2}{c}{Valid}		\multicolumn{2}{c}{Missing}		\multicolumn{2}{c}{Total}
	N	Percent	N	Percent	N	Percent
$ab^a	1767	39.2%	2743	60.8%	4510	100.0%

a. Dichotomy group tabulated at value 1.

$ab Frequencies

		Responses		Percent of Cases
		N	Percent	
$ab[a]	STRONG CHANCE OF SERIOUS DEFECT	1425	22.8%	80.6%
	WOMANS HEALTH SERIOUSLY ENDANGERED	1692	27.1%	95.8%
	MARRIED--WANTS NO MORE CHILDREN	818	13.1%	46.3%
	LOW INCOME--CANT AFFORD MORE CHILDREN	822	13.2%	46.5%
	PREGNANT AS RESULT OF RAPE	1483	23.8%	83.9%
Total		6240	100.0%	353.1%

a. Dichotomy group tabulated at value 1.

Note that the multiple-response command allows easy production of a table combining similar style variables counting a particular category or range. Above, it is easy to see the similarities and differences in percentages of those who support abortion in the listed circumstances.

3

Selecting and Sampling Cases

The SPSS Statistics software allows a user to draw a sample from a data set. This selection can be performed to take a random or a targeted sample.

Targeted Selection

For a particular analysis, researchers may not be interested in including all of the cases from a particular data file. There are numerous reasons why this might occur. For instance, if the researcher is only interested in studying characteristics of persons older than 21 years of age, then he or she will need to eliminate any cases in the data set of individuals who are 21 years of age or younger.

This condition comes up most often when using a secondary data set, one created by a third party, such as the General Social Survey (GSS). Since it was not originally custom-tailored to the needs of the researcher, that researcher will need to select the appropriate cases (as well as possibly recode variables, etc., as explained in Chapter 2: Transforming Variables).

To begin, select the following menus:

DATA → SELECT CASES . . .

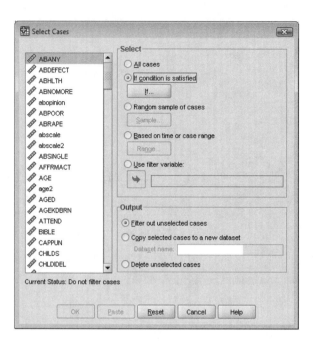

After choosing those menus, you will be given the "Select Cases" dialog box, as pictured above. Here, you can choose the types of respondents you would like to analyze and hence ignore those who do not fit your criteria for inclusion. To do so, click the "If" button under "Select . . . If condition is satisfied," after also choosing the corresponding radio button. Once you do that, you will be presented with the "Select Cases: If" dialog box, such as the one that follows:

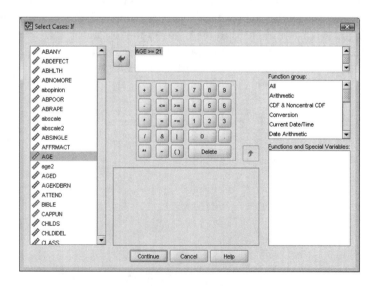

The functions in this box are similar in nature and operation to the functions in the compute dialog box used to compute new variables from existing data, described in Chapter 1. Suppose, as described earlier, the user wished to include only those respondents who were 21 years of age and older.

First, select the necessary variable(s) from the variable bank on the left. In this case, we need the variable "age." Click the arrow to move it to the right side of the dialog box. Now, click the " > = " (greater than or equals) sign and enter the number 21. Alternatively, you could have selected the ">" (greater than) button and entered the number 20. Since age is measured in whole years in the GSS, these two methods will return the same outcome.

Click the "Continue" button in the "Select Cases: If" dialog box, then click "OK" in the "Select Cases" dialog box. Next, see the data view window of your data set.

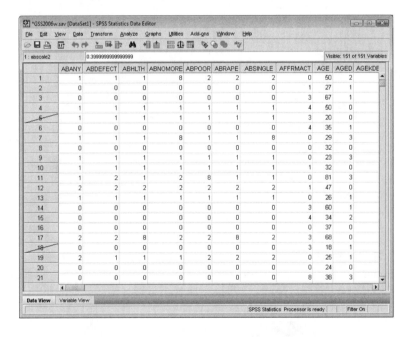

Note that some of the cases have a diagonal line through the SPSS case number at the left. This is how SPSS Statistics lets you know which cases will be omitted from any and all analyses performed, until the "Select Cases" function is changed or turned off.

Random Selection

Now, suppose the user wants to select a random group of cases from a particular data set. This can also be done by calling up the "Select Cases" dialog box:

DATA → SELECT CASES . . .

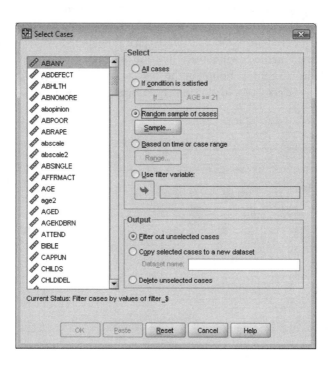

This time, click the "Sample" button after choosing the corresponding radio button "Select . . . Random sample of cases." You will then be given the "Select Cases: Random Sample" dialog box seen below:

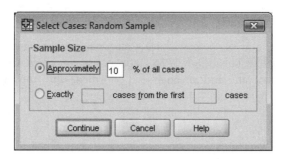

For this example, 10% of the cases will be chosen. SPSS Statistics uses the word *approximately* since not all data sets are necessarily divisible by the percentage that you choose and hence would not return a whole number of cases in the sample. Note that alternatively, you could select the other radio button and choose an exact number of cases from the first *N* number of cases, as the file is sorted. (Use the DATA → SORT CASES menu to change the way the cases in your data set are ordered in SPSS.)

Click "Continue," then click "OK" when you are taken back to the "Select Cases" dialog box. The image below shows the variable view "Data Editor" window after this action is performed:

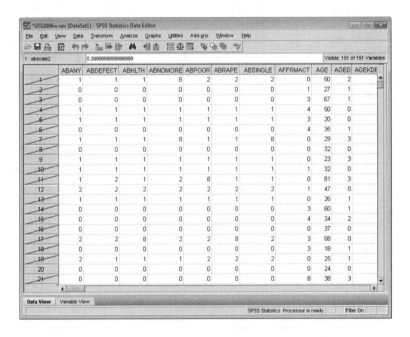

Many (approximately 90%) of the cases have a diagonal line through the SPSS case number at the left. Again, this is how SPSS lets you know which cases will be omitted from any and all analyses performed, until the "Select Cases" function is changed or turned off.

Selecting Cases for Inclusion in a New Data Set

Up to this point, we have selected cases from a data set while having SPSS ignore those cases that were not selected for inclusion. It is also possible to have SPSS create a new data file that contains only the cases that have been selected.

The process of case selection is identical. The difference is in the "Output" section of the dialog box:

DATA → SELECT CASES . . .

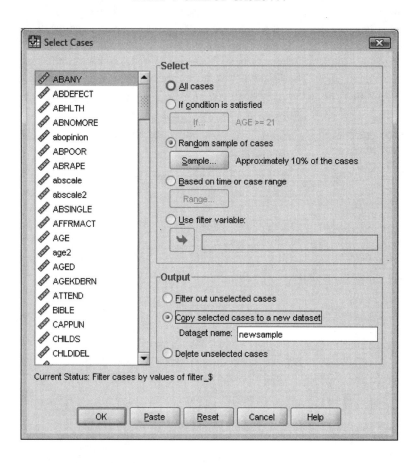

Choose the radio button for "Copy selected cases to a new dataset." Then enter a name for your new file. It will be stored in the default directory as an SPSS Statistics *.sav file. The advantage to choosing this option is that you can work with the subset data file without risk of altering the full original data file.

4

Organization and Presentation of Information

In this chapter, basic methods of data description will be exhibited. This information will include frequency distributions, measures of central tendency, and measures of variability. Presentation can be made in table, chart, and graph forms.

Measures of Central Tendency and Variability

To quickly produce a table with basic descriptive statistics about a variable or variables, select the following menus.

ANALYZE → DESCRIPTIVE STATISTICS → DESCRIPTIVES . . .

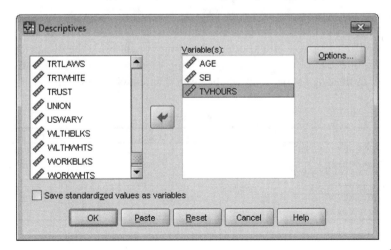

By clicking on the "Options" button at the upper right-hand corner of the "Descriptives" dialog box, you will be given another dialog box that will allow you to choose which basic descriptive information will be produced by SPSS.

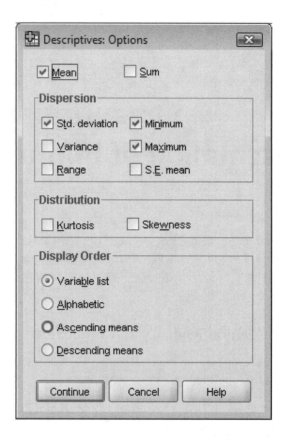

Select the boxes, leaving a checkmark next to those statistics that you would like to request. You also have the option of choosing the display order; choose one of the four options. After clicking "Continue" in this dialog box and "OK" in the original one, you will be given the following SPSS output.

Descriptive Statistics

	N	Minimum	Maximum	Mean	Std. Deviation
AGE OF RESPONDENT	4492	18	89	47.14	16.894
RESPONDENT SOCIOECONOMIC INDEX	4242	17.1	97.2	49.410	19.5995
HOURS PER DAY WATCHING TV	1987	0	24	2.94	2.286
Valid N (listwise)	1868				

Note that the sample size and the four measures that were selected have been presented in separate columns. Variables are listed in the rows of the table output.

While that method of getting basic descriptive information is very quick and easy, it is possible to get more detailed descriptive information about variables in a data set. Note that the previous method will NOT allow you to obtain the median. One can obtain information about measures of central tendency (*including the median*) and variability, as well as obtaining actual frequency distribution tables.

Frequency Distributions

Using the same variables as in the previous example, select the following menus.

ANALYZE → DESCRIPTIVE STATISTICS → FREQUENCIES . . .

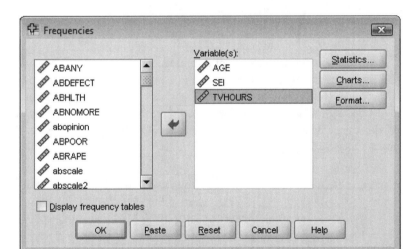

For now, make sure that the "Display frequency tables" box is *unchecked*. The three selected variables, age, sei, and tvhours, are all scale variables. Therefore, the frequency distribution tables would have too many categories and be too long to be of any real use. One must be cognizant of the level of measurement and categorization of variables before selecting tables.

To choose which statistical information to request, click the "Statistics" button, and you will be presented with the following dialog box.

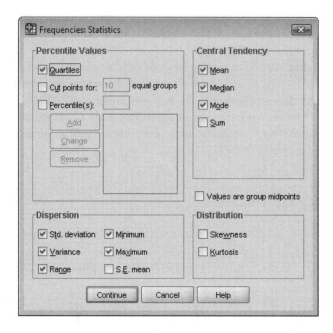

Here, you can choose measures of central tendency (mean, median, and/or mode) and measures of variability. Quartiles are useful for computing the interquartile range (IQR). You can also select any percentile for computation as well, depending on your specific needs. Based on the above dialog boxes, the following output will be provided once you click "Continue" then "OK" in the original dialog box.

Statistics

		AGE OF RESPONDENT	RESPONDENT SOCIO-ECONOMIC INDEX	HOURS PER DAY WATCHING TV
N	Valid	4492	4242	1987
	Missing	18	268	2523
Mean		47.14	49.410	2.94
Median		46.00	42.200	2.00
Mode		47	63.5	2
Std. Deviation		16.894	19.5995	2.286
Variance		285.416	384.139	5.225
Range		71	80.1	24
Minimum		18	17.1	0
Maximum		89	97.2	24
Percentiles	25	34.00	32.775	1.00
	50	46.00	42.200	2.00
	75	59.00	64.100	4.00

Now, perform the same menu function with a different variable.

ANALYZE → DESCRIPTIVES → FREQUENCIES . . .

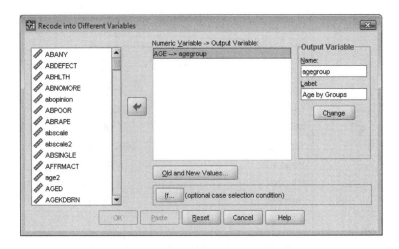

First, remove the variables that were there by clicking the "Reset" button. Now, select "age2," the recoded age dichotomy variable, and move it into the "Variable(s)" box. Click the "Charts" button. You will be given a subdialog box as follows.

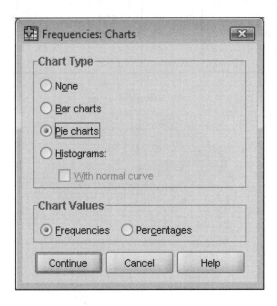

Choose the "Pie charts" radio button and "Frequencies." [Of course, depending on your needs and the level of measurement of your variable(s), you could select any of these types of charts.] Then click "Continue" and then "OK" in the original dialog box. The information below represents the output that SPSS will provide.

Statistics

age 50 & over or not

N	Valid	4492
	Missing	18
Mean		.4159
Median		.0000
Mode		.00
Std. Deviation		.49292
Variance		.243
Range		1.00
Percentiles	25	.0000
	50	.0000
	75	1.0000

age 50 & over or not

		Frequency	Percent	Valid Percent	Cumulative Percent
Valid	Aged 49 or less	2624	58.2	58.4	58.4
	Aged 50 or over	1868	41.4	41.6	100.0
	Total	4492	99.6	100.0	
Missing	System	18	.4		
Total		4510	100.0		

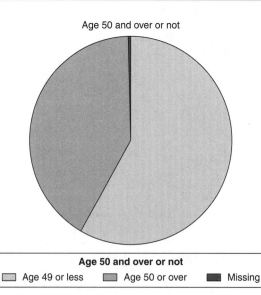

Age 50 and over or not

Age 50 and over or not
Age 49 or less   Age 50 or over   Missing

While this is one way to obtain some of the chart and graph options, more detailed options and optimized interfaces for producing charts and graphs are explained in the next chapter.

Now, suppose that you want to produce a frequency distribution for age beyond just the dichotomy that was demonstrated in the previous example. It is not feasible to run the frequency command/menus using age since a virtually useless table listing all ages in the data file will be generated.

To present a useful frequency distribution, you should divide the interval ratio variable, age, into meaningful or otherwise appropriate categories. Take, for instance, the following example where age is divided into ranges according to decade. Bear in mind that the General Social Survey (GSS) contains responses only from those 18 years of age and older. First, use the following menus to recode age into agegroup (see Chapter 2 for more detail on recoding):

TRANSFORM → RECODE → INTO DIFFERENT VARIABLES . . .

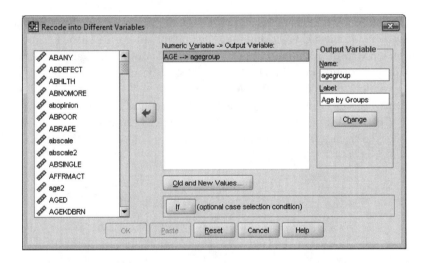

Select the original variable from the variable list on the left and move it into the "Numeric Variable -> Output Variable" area. On the right side of the dialog box, be sure to name the new variable (here, the new name is age group) and provide a label if desired. Now, click the "Old and New Values" button. The following dialog box will be presented:

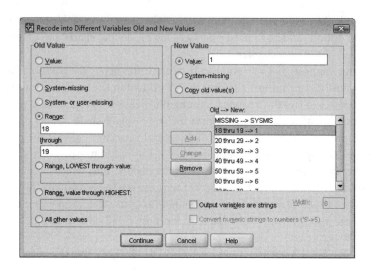

Here, enter the old values and ranges on the left in conjunction with the new value on the right, clicking the "Add" button after each entry. For more details, review the recoding section of Chapter 2: Transforming Variables. After all of the old and new values have been added, click the "Continue" button in this window, then "OK" in the "Recode into Different Variables" dialog box. The new variable will be displayed in the SPSS Statistics "Data Editor" window.

Click the "Variable View" tab and find the newly created variable. In the "Values" cell, click the button with three dots. You will be given the following dialog box.

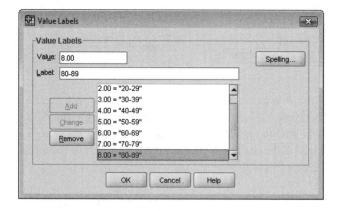

Enter the appropriate labels, as done in the example above. Then click "OK." This will record the labels onto the variable.

Next, request a frequency distribution for the newly structured variable. To do so, click the following menus:

ANALYZE → DESCRIPTIVE STATISTICS → FREQUENCIES . . .

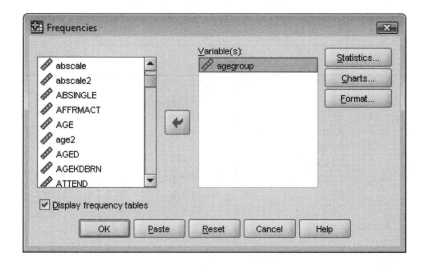

When given the above dialog box, move the variable of interest from the list on the left into the "Variable(s)" box. For a visual representation of the distribution, select the "Charts . . ." button and see the dialog box that follows.

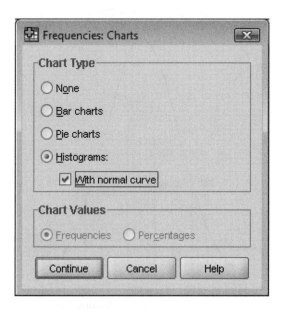

Click the radio button next to "Histograms" and check the box for "With normal curve." This will produce a histogram with an overlay of a normal curve for reference. Click "Continue" here, then click "OK" in the prior dialog box. SPSS will generate the following output consisting of an easy to understand frequency table and a histogram.

Age by Groups

		Frequency	Percent	Valid Percent	Cumulative Percent
Valid	18–19	16	1.1	1.1	1.1
	20–29	275	18.3	18.4	19.5
	30–39	323	21.5	21.6	41.0
	40–49	291	19.4	19.5	60.5
	50–59	234	15.6	15.6	76.1
	60–69	170	11.3	11.4	87.5
	70–79	123	8.2	8.2	95.7
	80–89	64	4.3	4.3	100.0
	Total	1496	99.7	100.0	
Missing	System	4	.3		
Total		1500	100.0		

Note that by inspecting the "Valid Percent" column, one can readily get a sense of the distribution due to the manageable number of categories (rows) in the table. This same information is provided graphically in the histogram that follows.

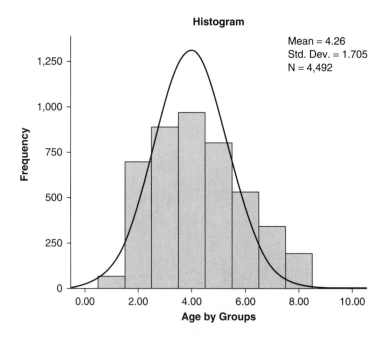

Histogram

Mean = 4.26
Std. Dev. = 1.705
N = 4,492

5

Charts and Graphs

In this chapter, the techniques for producing a number of useful graphics will be explained. A number of other chart and graph options are not explained in this section, although they are contained within the "Graph" menu and can be explored with knowledge of how to use the other SPSS Statistics graph functions along with statistical and research methods background.

Most of the charts and graphs discussed in this section, as well as those not covered in this book, can be "double-clicked" in the "Output Editor." After double-clicking, the object opens in a new window that allows editing of text, colors, graphics, additions of other features, and even other variables.

From the SPSS Statistics editor window, the graphs, charts, and tables that are produced can be selected and copied (Control + C or Apple + C) then pasted (Control + V or Apple + V, or "Paste Special") into a word-processing program such as Microsoft Word, a publishing program, or a Web design program.

Boxplot

A boxplot is a visual representation of the frequency distribution of a variable showing shape, central tendency, and variability of a distribution. It can also be called a box-and-whisker diagram. To produce a boxplot:

GRAPHS → CHART BUILDER . . .

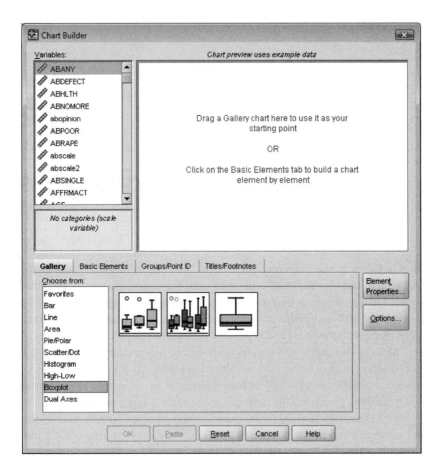

In this example, we will draw a simple boxplot for one variable, age. After being presented with a dialog box such as the one above, select "Boxplot" from the gallery at the bottom of this window. SPSS presents three choices for the boxplot. For this example, we will select the third choice, examining just one variable. Drag and drop the selection into the open area toward the top right side of this window.

Now, you will need to select a variable from the list on the left to drag into the area marked "X-Axis?" SPSS requires a variable to be dragged to that area to compute and draw the boxplot. Once you do this, the screen will look like the one that follows.

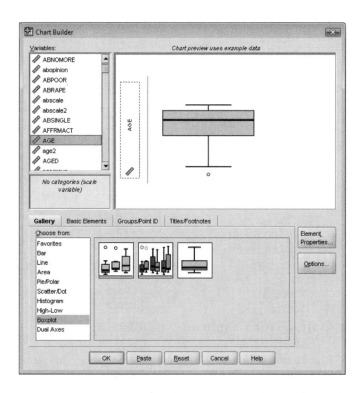

The "Element Properties" window will automatically open. Here, you have options to set the scale range for the graph, as well as the label for the X-Axis in this case. Labels, titles, legends, and so on can all be edited in the output window of SPSS as well (see Chapter 10: Editing Output).

After clicking "OK" in the Chart Builder dialog box, SPSS will produce the boxplot in the "Output Viewer" window. Information about the distribution of the variable is contained in the boxplot. The upper and lower boundaries of the box itself represent Q3 (the 75th percentile) and Q1 (the 25th percentile), respectively. Values correspond to the scale on the left axis of the figure. Therefore, the box itself shows the interquartile (IQR). The line inside the box is drawn at the 50th percentile. The lines extending above and below the box are referred to as whiskers. At the end of the top whisker, the maximum score is marked. The minimum value can be found at the end of the lower whisker.

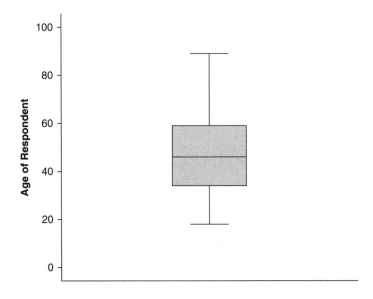

Legacy Options for Graphs (Boxplot Example)

The SPSS Chart Builder is a newer feature in SPSS Statistics. The option to create charts and graphs using the previous system remains in the program and can be particularly useful for quick creation of certain output, if the researcher knows exactly what type of visual display is desired in advance.

GRAPHS → LEGACY DIALOGS → BOXPLOT . . .

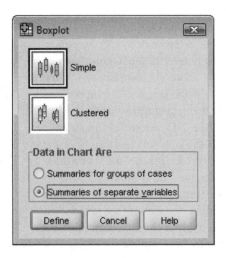

In this example, we will draw a simple boxplot for one variable, age, as before with the SPSS Chart Builder. Click "Simple" and select the button for "Summaries of Separate Variables." Then click the "Define" button. You will be given another dialog box.

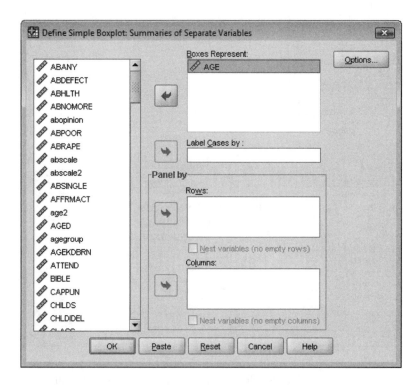

In this dialog box, move the variable(s) of interest into the "Boxes Represent" location. Click "OK," and SPSS will provide the boxplot(s) that you have requested. It will be nearly identical to the output provided by the Chart Builder option, only varying in ways related to formatting that is selected.

Scatterplot

A scatterplot is a useful graph to display the relationship between two scale, or interval ratio, variables. To create a scatterplot, use these menu directions:

GRAPHS → CHART BUILDER . . .

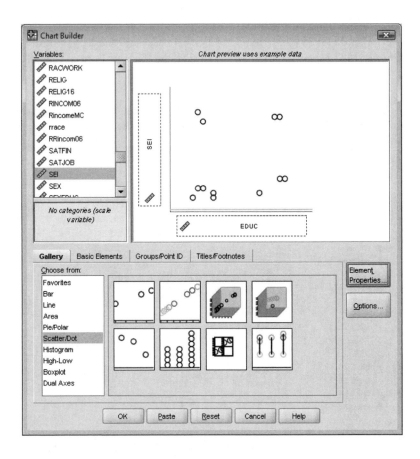

In the Chart Builder window, select "Scatter/Dot" from the gallery. Drag and drop the type of scatterplot you would like to produce into the preview pane. For this example, choose the first option and drag it to the preview area. Once there, you will need to select variables for both the X- and Y-axes. For this example, we will plot socioeconomic index by years of education. Drag the "SEI" variable from the "Variables" bank on the left into the Y-Axis location. Then drag the "educ" variable from the "Variables" bank into the X-Axis location. You can use the "Element Properties" window to change the scale of the graph, edit labels, and so on.

Click "OK" in the Chart Builder, and SPSS will provide the scatterplot in the Output Viewer window, as illustrated below. In the graph for SEI by years of education, there does appear to be an upward trend. Note also that the data points all fall along vertical lines due to the nature of the variable education, which has been categorized into a discrete number of years (not allowing for 13.5 years, for instance). In the case of a true continuously measured variable, those distinct vertical lines would not show up in the scatterplot.

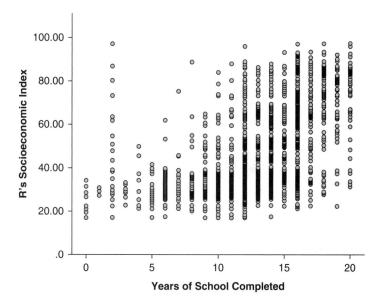

Legacy Scatterplot

To use the legacy option, the method from prior versions of SPSS software, for creating a scatterplot, you should use the following menus and proceed using the same information that was entered using the Chart Builder option.

GRAPHS → LEGACY DIALOGS → SCATTER/DOT . . .

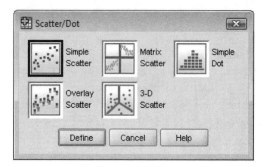

Then, click "Simple Scatter" for our example. Note the other types of scatterplots available to you depending on the nature of the variables you wish to graph. Click "Define." You will then be presented with the Simple Scatterplot dialog box, such as the one below.

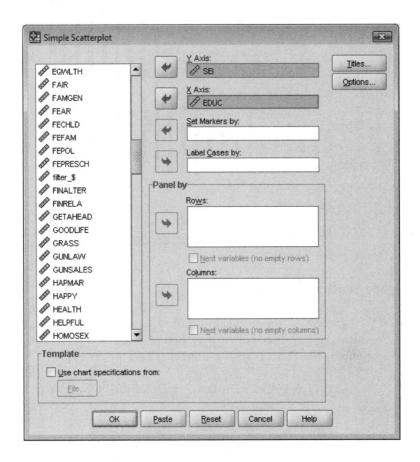

Select variables for the X- and Y-axes. In this example, SEI has been selected for the Y-axis (dependent variable), and years of education has been chosen for the X-axis (independent variable). Once you click "OK," SPSS will produce a scatterplot nearly identical to the one provided using the Chart Builder option.

Histogram

A histogram displays a graphic representation of the distribution of a single scale variable. This is a bar graph that can be used with variables at the interval and ratio levels. The bars touch. The width of the bars represents the width of the intervals, and the height of the bars represents the frequency of each interval. To create a histogram, follow these menus:

GRAPHS → CHART BUILDER . . .

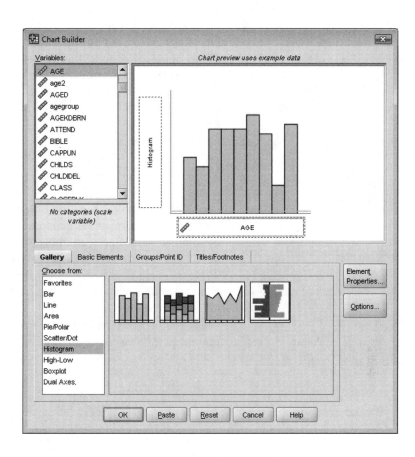

In the Chart Builder window, select "Histogram" from the gallery at the bottom of the window. Then choose the appropriate option. Use the first option. Now, move the variable of interest into the Chart Preview area. In this case, age was chosen.

Next, in the "Element Properties" window, making sure that you are editing properties of "Bar1," check the box that is associated with "Display normal curve." Then, click "OK" in the Chart Builder window.

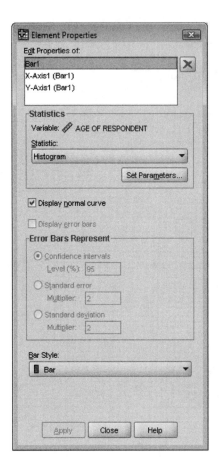

The SPSS output is shown below. The histogram is displayed, and an overlay of a normal curve has been added, per our request.

To produce a stacked histogram, displaying stacked bars of one variable's distribution according to categories of another variable, select the second histogram option. Add the variable of interest, age, to the X-axis. Then, move the variable by which you would like the bars divided into the "Stack: set color" box.

Note that you cannot divide bars by a variable that is "scale" according to SPSS. Even if it is a nominal variable, you cannot move it to the "Stack" location unless SPSS recognizes it as nominal or ordinal. To change a variable from scale to nominal or ordinal (assuming it is indeed not a scale variable), go to the SPSS Statistics "Variable View" window. Find the variable you wish to change, and under the "Measure" column, click and then select the new level of measurement from the pull-down choices.

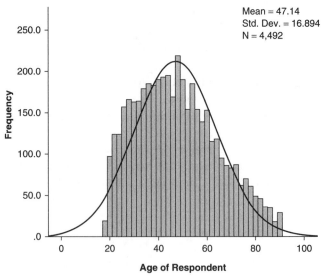

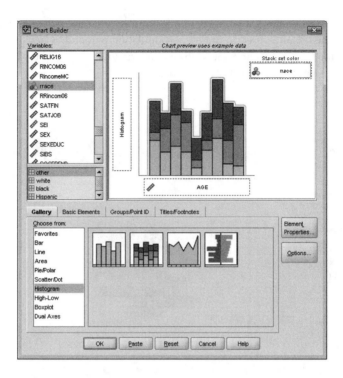

Click "OK," and the following output will be produced in the SPSS Statistics Output Viewer.

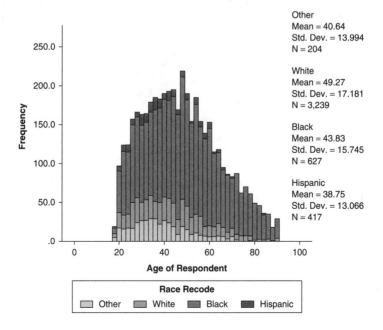

A two-sided horizontal histogram is another often used graphic in social science classes, often used to present a "population pyramid." Click the fourth choice for this option and move the main axis variable and the variable to define the categories (sides) of the graph.

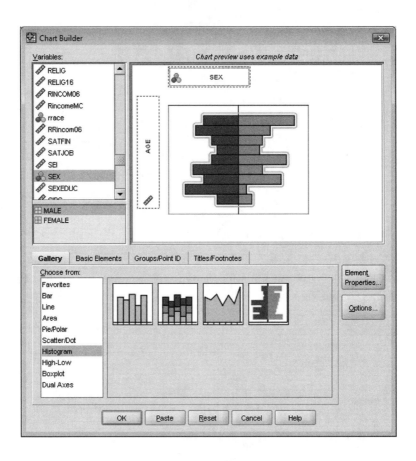

If you use "AGE" as the distribution variable and wish to divide the distribution by "SEX," the following output will be returned after clicking "OK."

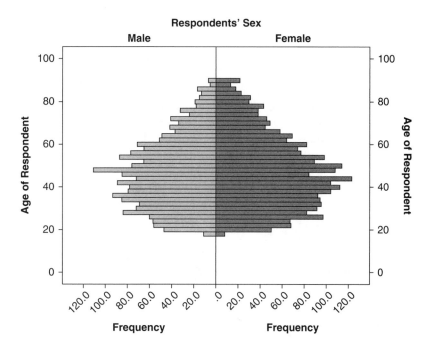

Note that the third option in the histogram gallery of the Chart Builder is a variation of a frequency polygon that can be created using the same technique as the first histogram option.

To produce histograms using the older version SPSS method, select the following menus and enter the information about your variables and the type of graph you would like to produce.

GRAPHS → LEGACY DIALOGS → HISTOGRAM . . .

Bar Graph

Usage of bar graphs is common and varied. SPSS Statistics provides many ways of using bar graphs to illustrate information. Much like in Microsoft Excel or other spreadsheet and data graphics programs, SPSS produces bar charts in a number of different ways. It is possible to create standard bar charts, as well as clustered or stacked bar charts. To produce a bar graph, use these menus:

GRAPHS → CHART BUILDER . . .

You will be given a small dialog box, which precedes the main "Bar Chart" dialog boxes. For this example, click "Simple," then click the "Define" button. Now you will be given the "Define Simple Bar" dialog box and can enter the information to produce the graph.

Be sure that your variable is recognized by SPSS as having the correct level of measurement. For instance, if you have a nominal variable, and it is coded in SPSS as scale, then the bar graph option will automatically turn the bar graph into a histogram.

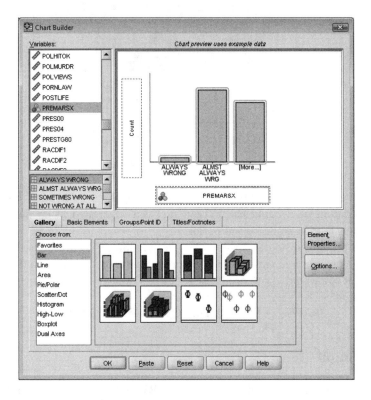

In this example, select "N of cases," indicating that the frequency count will be displayed. Then select the variable for graphing from the list on the left and click the arrow moving it into the "Category Axis" box. Then click "OK." Following is an image of the graph that SPSS will produce.

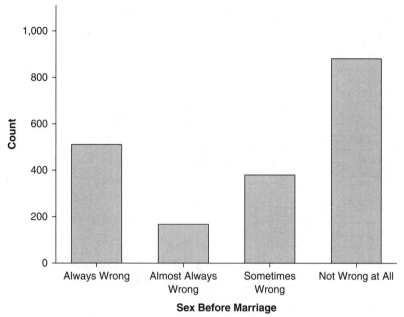

Note that a title and annotation have been added. More information about how to edit graphs can be found in Chapter 10: Editing Output.

One might wish to produce clustered bar graphs when comparing the information, such as that shown above about beliefs concerning premarital sex, across categories of things such as gender, race/ethnicity, or age groups. In the example that follows, we examine beliefs about premarital sex by gender. With a clustered bar graph in this case, it is beneficial to graph the percentage of respondents versus the number of respondents, so that the relative bar lengths can be more easily compared within categories of the dependent variable. So, select the following menus:

GRAPHS → CHART BUILDER . . .

Now, select the "Clustered" option, as seen in the following image (it is the second choice in the "Bar" gallery). Then drag it to the chart preview area.

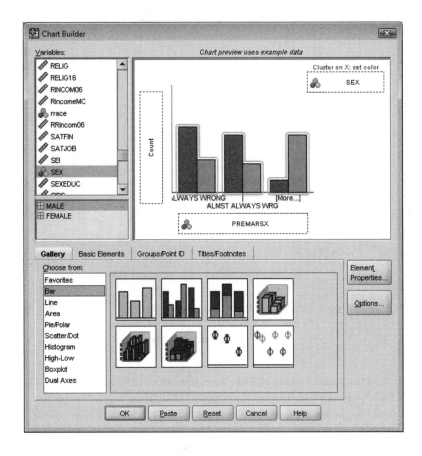

You have the option at this point to select the "Titles/Footnotes" tab, where you will be presented with spaces to easily enter that information. In this example, you will notice that the output (below) has been edited to include a title and footnote. You can also add this information later in the SPSS Output Viewer window by double-clicking the object and working with the editing tools there; for more information, see Chapter 10: Editing Output.

Now, tell SPSS with which variables you will be working. Move the dependent variable, premarsx, into the "X-Axis" box in the chart preview area. Next, move the independent variable, sex, from the variable list on the left side into the "Cluster on X" box in the chart preview area.

Next, you will need to select "Element Properties" and make sure to change the bar graph option from count to percentage, and elect the option for percentage, which uses all of the bars of the same color (total for that grouping category) as the denominator.

Now, click "Continue" in this box, then click "OK" in the Chart Builder window. SPSS Statistics will produce the following output.

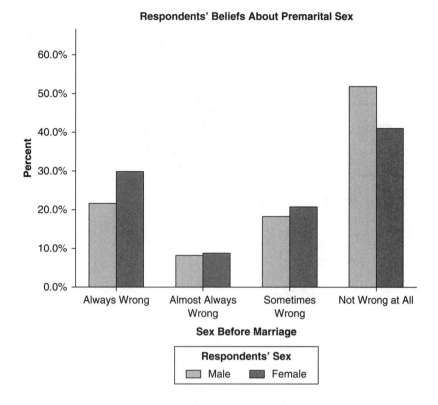

It is readily apparent from the bar chart prepared by SPSS that women tend to take a less favorable view of premarital sex than do men. Notice that a larger percentage of the women than the men who were in the sample responded "always wrong." Likewise, a smaller percentage of the women responded "not wrong at all."

To produce bar graphs using the older version SPSS method, select the following menus and enter the information about your variables and the type of graph you would like to produce.

GRAPHS → LEGACY DIALOGS → BAR . . .

Pie Chart

Pie charts are circular graphs with slices that represent the proportion of the total contained within each category. To produce a pie chart, select the following menus:

GRAPHS → CHART BUILDER . . .

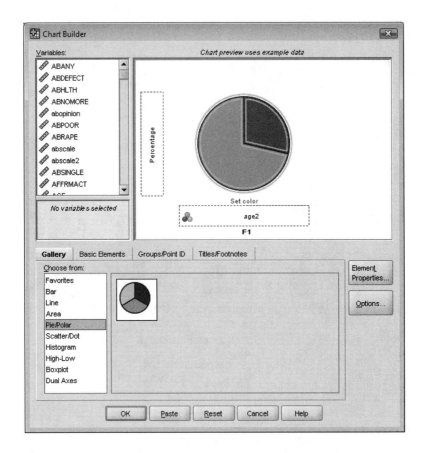

Reminder: SPSS Statistics will not allow you to use variables that it recognizes as "scale" to draw a pie chart. If the variable you wish to draw is not scale, you may change the recognition setting for that variable in the SPSS "Variable View" window under the "Measure" column.

For this example, use age2, the recoded version of age, reducing the data into a dichotomy: two categories. A pie chart is useful for nominal and many ordinal variables, particularly dichotomies. It would be of little or no use to create a pie chart for the original age variable since there would be too many slices from which to make much sense.

First, click "Pie/Polar" from the gallery at the bottom of the Chart Builder window. Then drag the only available option to the chart preview area. Now, move the age2 variable to the box underneath the pie chart.

Again, note that you have the option to select the "Titles/Footnotes" tab, where you will be presented with spaces to easily enter that information. In this example, you will notice that the output (below) has been edited to include a title and footnote. You can also add this information later in the SPSS Output Viewer window by double-clicking the object and working with the editing tools there; for more information, see Chapter 10: Editing Output.

Next, click on "Element Properties" and choose "Polar interval1." In the "Statistics" box, select percentage. There will only be one choice when clicking the "Set Parameters" button: Grand Total.

Now, click the "OK" button in the Chart Builder window. The following graphic will be produced in the SPSS Statistics Output Viewer window.

The SPSS output above provides descriptive (percentage) information in visual form for the variable selected, age2, age distribution reduced into two categories.

To produce pie charts using the older version SPSS method, select the following menus and enter the information about your variables and the type of chart you would like to produce.

GRAPHS → LEGACY DIALOGS
→ PIE . . .

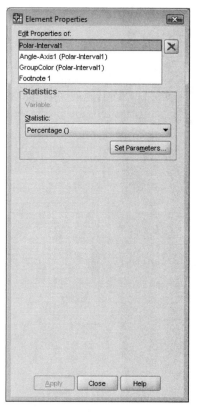

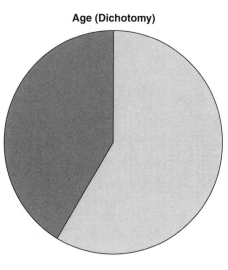

Age (Dichotomy)

Age 50 and over or not	
☐ Age 49 or less	■ Age 50 or over

Additional Graphic Capabilities in SPSS Statistics

Using the SPSS Statistics Chart Builder, you are able to create additional types of graphics, not covered in this chapter (such as line graphs and graphs with dual axes), by selecting those templates from the gallery in the Chart Builder window. The options for patterns, clustering, and so on can be followed from the instructions for the graphs discussed in this chapter.

GRAPHS → CHART BUILDER . . .

6

Cross-Tabulation and Measures of Association for Nominal and Ordinal Variables

The most basic type of cross-tabulation (crosstabs) is used to analyze relationships between two variables. This allows a researcher to explore the relationship between variables by examining the intersections of categories of each of the variables involved. The simplest type of cross-tabulation is bivariate analysis, an analysis of two variables. However, the analysis can be expanded beyond that.

Bivariate Analysis

By example, follow these menus to conduct a cross-tabulation of two variables:

ANALYZE → DESCRIPTIVES STATISTICS → CROSSTABS . . .

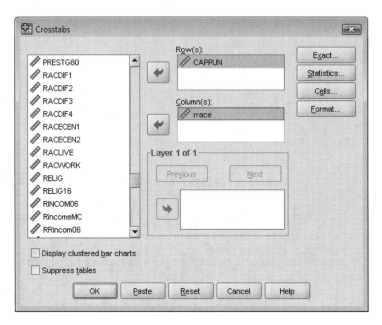

After selecting those menus, you will be presented with a dialog box such as the one above. Here, you will have the opportunity to select the row and column variables for the bivariate table. As is customary, it is recommended that you choose the independent variable as the column variable. Above, cappun (view on capital punishment/the death penalty) has been selected for the row variable, and rrace (recoded version of respondents' race) has been chosen as the column variable. We use rrace since the number of categories has been collapsed to four. This

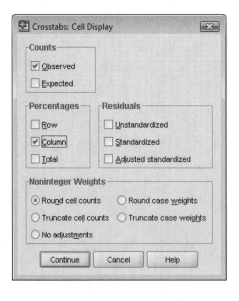

makes it easier to interpret data from cross-tabulations when the number of categories is kept smaller. Next, click on the "Cells" button to choose options about what information will be given in the output table.

Be sure that the "Column" box is checked under "Percentages." This will make sure that you have information from the appropriate perspective to analyze your variables based on which is the predictor. Click "Continue" in the "Cell Display" dialog box, then "OK" in the original "Crosstabs" dialog box. The table that follows comes from the output produced by following the aforementioned steps.

FAVOR OR OPPOSE DEATH PENALTY FOR MURDER * Race Recode Crosstabulation

			Race Recode				Total
			other	white	black	Hispanic	
FAVOR OR OPPOSE DEATH PENALTY FOR MURDER	FAVOR	Count	83	1508	159	134	1884
		% within Race Recode	66.4%	73.3%	42.4%	52.5%	67.0%
	OPPOSE	Count	42	549	216	121	928
		% within Race Recode	33.6%	26.7%	57.6%	47.5%	33.0%
Total		Count	125	2057	375	255	2812
		% within Race Recode	100.0%	100.0%	100.0%	100.0%	100.0%

Based on the information in the table, it is easy to see that there is some sort of relationship between the variables of interest in this case. Note that by looking at the percentages across the columns (categories of the independent variable), one can see that there are differences in opinion about the death penalty by race. According to these General Social Survey (GSS) data, Whites and others are more likely to favor the death penalty than Blacks or Hispanics.

Adding Another Variable or Dimension to the Analysis

Suppose we want to further explore the bivariate relationship that we briefly examined in the preceding section. By adding another variable, such as respondent's sex, we can further explore how opinions about capital punishment are held in the United States. One way that we can perform this type of analysis is to split our data file by respondent's sex. At that point, any analysis that we do will be performed across the categories of the variable with which we have split the data set.

To split the data file by respondent's sex, use these menus:

DATA → SPLIT FILE . . .

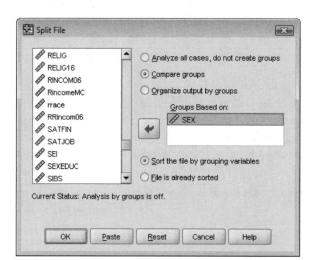

You will be given a "Split File" dialog box such as the one above. Here, choose the "Compare groups" radio button. This will brighten the "Groups Based on" box and allow you to now move variables into that box, which will then be used to split the data file. Find "sex" from the variable bank on the left and move it over into the "Groups Based on" box. It is often a good idea to make sure that the file is sorted by grouping variables, although this is not necessary. Click "OK."

SPSS will now perform the split file function. You will know that the data file has been split by the indicator in the lower right-hand window of the data editor. It will say "Split File On."

Now, go back to the crosstabs menu and perform the same operations that were done in the previous section. (The variables and setting should remain the same from before, so unless you have restarted SPSS in between, it will be just a matter of choosing "OK" once the dialog box appears.)

ANALYZE → DECRIPTIVES → CROSSTABS . . .

FAVOR OR OPPOSE DEATH PENALTY FOR MURDER * Race Recode Crosstabulation

				Race Recode				
RESPONDENTS SEX				other	white	black	Hispanic	Total
MALE	FAVOR OR OPPOSE DEATH PENALTY FOR MURDER	FAVOR	Count	33	710	64	68	875
			% within Race Recode	64.7%	77.2%	47.4%	54.0%	71.0%
		OPPOSE	Count	18	210	71	58	357
			% within Race Recode	35.3%	22.8%	52.6%	46.0%	29.0%
	Total		Count	51	920	135	126	1232
			% within Race Recode	100.0%	100.0%	100.0%	100.0%	100.0%
FEMALE	FAVOR OR OPPOSE DEATH PENALTY FOR MURDER	FAVOR	Count	50	798	95	66	1009
			% within Race Recode	67.6%	70.2%	39.6%	51.2%	63.9%
		OPPOSE	Count	24	339	145	63	571
			% within Race Recode	32.4%	29.8%	60.4%	48.8%	36.1%
	Total		Count	74	1137	240	129	1580
			% within Race Recode	100.0%	100.0%	100.0%	100.0%	100.0%

The table above will be presented as part of the output that SPSS returns. While it is similar to the table given in the prior section, note that it has twice as many cells. It has been split into two tables, one for men and one for women. In this instance, among other things, it can be seen from the table that Hispanic females have the highest percentage of all categories of men and women who "favor the death penalty for murder." In all other racial categories, men tended to be more likely to favor the death penalty. By adding this new dimension, we were able to obtain some additional insight into public opinion on this matter. See your statistics or research methods book(s) for more details.

Measures of Association for Nominal and Ordinal Variables

PRE statistics allow us to determine the proportional reduction of error achieved by adding one or more variables to an analysis (even if it is the initial independent variable). "PRE measures are derived by comparing the errors made in predicting the dependent variable while ignoring the independent variable with errors made when making predictions that use information about the independent variable" (Frankfort-Nachmias & Leon-Guerrero, 2006). For nominal variables, a PRE statistic that we can use is lambda. For details on how lambda is specifically calculated, see Chapter 12 of *Social Statistics for a Diverse Society* (Frankfort-Nachmias & Leon-Guerrero, 2009).

Lambda

Lambda is a measure of association for nominal variables. It ranges from 0 to 1. When lambda equals 0, then there is no association; none of the variation in the dependent variable can be explained by the variation in the independent variable. When lambda equals 1, it is a perfect (deterministic) association; 100% (all) of the variation in the dependent variable can be explained by the variation of the independent variable.

To compute lambda for the relationship between race and view on capital punishment, begin again by selecting the cross-tabulation menu:

ANALYZE → DESCRIPTIVES → CROSSTABS . . .

Now, when presented with the "Crosstabs" dialog box and after entering the variables of interest, select the "Statistics" button. You will be given the following dialog box:

Under the "Nominal" heading, select "Lambda." This will instruct SPSS to add lambda to the things it will present in the output. Now, click "Continue" in the "Statistics" dialog box, then "OK" in the prior dialog box. In the following, you will find an image from the output SPSS would produce:

Directional Measures

			Value	Asymp. Std. Error[a]	Approx. T[b]	Approx. Sig.
Nominal by Nominal	Lambda	Symmetric	.034	.011	2.948	.003
		FAVOR OR OPPOSE DEATH PENALTY FOR MURDER Dependent	.061	.020	2.948	.003
		Race Recode Dependent	.000	.000	[c]	[c]
	Goodman and Kruskal tau	FAVOR OR OPPOSE DEATH PENALTY FOR MURDER Dependent	.058	.009		.000[d]
		Race Recode Dependent	.035	.006		.000[d]

a. Not assuming the null hypothesis.

b. Using the asymptotic standard error assuming the null hypothesis.

c. Cannot be computed because the asymptotic standard error equals zero.

d. Based on chi-square approximation

Typically, lambda is presented as an asymmetrical measure of association as is the case in *Social Statistics for a Diverse Society* (Frankfort-Nachmias & Leon-Guerrero, 2006). Given that, the value of lambda to be used can be found in the "value" column in the row indicating the correct dependent variable. In this case, cappun (favor or oppose death penalty for murder) is the appropriate dependent variable. We see that lambda is 0.013 and that it is not statistically significant ($p = .756$).

Gamma and Somers' *d*

Gamma and Somers' *d* are both measures of association for ordinal (and dichotomous) variables. Gamma, sometimes referred to as Goodman and Kruskal's gamma, is a symmetrical measure of association. Somers' *d* is an asymmetrical measure; SPSS Statistics uses the term *directional measure* to describe asymmetrical measures. Both gamma and Somers' *d* can take on values from –1 to +1. A value of +1 indicates that there is a deterministic and positive association, such that all of the variation in the dependent variable is accounted for by the variation in the independent variable. A value of –1 indicates, again, that there is a deterministic association but that it is negative. While all of the variation in the dependent variable is accounted for by the variation in the independent variable, the association is in the opposite (negative) direction. When gamma or Somers' *d* equals 0, that indicates that there is no association; none of the variation in the dependent variable can be explained by the variation in the independent variable. Of course, the closer the value of either of these measures is to zero, the weaker the association. The closer the value is to +1 or –1, the stronger the association, in the respective direction.

To compute other measures of association, such as gamma and Somers' *d*, use the following guidelines.

ANALYZE → DESCRIPTIVE STATISTICS → CROSSTABS

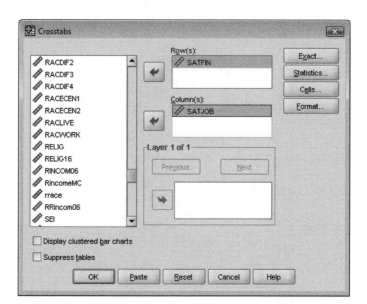

You will be given a "Crosstabs" dialog box. For this example, select satfin as the row variable and satjob as the column variable. Satfin is the variable representing how satisfied the respondent was with her or his financial situation. Satjob reveals the level of satisfaction that the respondent feels about her or his job or housework.

Now, click the "Cells" button.

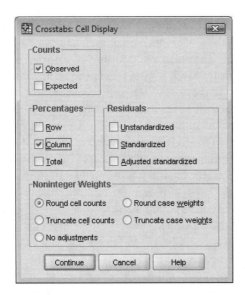

In the "Cells" dialog box, make sure that "Observed" counts are selected and that "Column" percentages have been requested. Now, click "Continue." You will be returned to the "Crosstabs" dialog box. Here, click the "Statistics" button. You will be given the following dialog box:

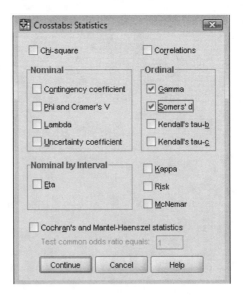

In this box, select gamma and Somers' *d*. Click "Continue" and then click "OK" once you are returned to the original "Crosstabs" dialog box. The tables below come from the output that SPSS will create:

SATISFACTION WITH FINANCIAL SITUATION * JOB OR HOUSEWORK Crosstabulation

			JOB OR HOUSEWORK				
			VERY SATISFIED	MOD. SATISFIED	A LITTLE DISSAT	VERY DISSATISFIED	Total
SATISFACTION WITH FINANCIAL SITUATION	SATISFIED	Count	379	192	30	13	614
		% within JOB OR HOUSEWORK	35.6%	23.4%	15.6%	14.6%	28.3%
	MORE OR LESS	Count	479	405	82	26	992
		% within JOB OR HOUSEWORK	45.0%	49.3%	42.7%	29.2%	45.8%
	NOT AT ALL SAT	Count	207	224	80	50	561
		% within JOB OR HOUSEWORK	19.4%	27.3%	41.7%	56.2%	25.9%
Total		Count	1065	821	192	89	2167
		% within JOB OR HOUSEWORK	100.0%	100.0%	100.0%	100.0%	100.0%

Note that the standard cross-tabulation is produced above and gives an overview by column percents of the relationship between the two variables.

Directional Measures

			Value	Asymp. Std. Error[a]	Approx. T[b]	Approx. Sig.
Ordinal by Ordinal	Somers' d	Symmetric	.191	.019	9.897	.000
		SATISFACTION WITH FINANCIAL SITUATION Dependent	.197	.020	9.897	.000
		JOB OR HOUSEWORK Dependent	.185	.019	9.897	.000

a. Not assuming the null hypothesis.

b. Using the asymptotic standard error assuming the null hypothesis.

The value for Somers' *d* is located in the value column in the row with the appropriate variable listed as the dependent variable. (Note that since Somers' *d* is asymmetrical, the two values given, where the dependent variables are different, turn out to be different.) Somers' *d* is statistically significant in this case ($p = .000$).

Symmetric Measures

		Value	Asymp. Std. Error[a]	Approx. T[b]	Approx. Sig.
Ordinal by Ordinal	Gamma	.303	.029	9.897	.000
N of Valid Cases		2167			

a. Not assuming the null hypothesis.

b. Using the asymptotic standard error assuming the null hypothesis.

Above, note the value for gamma: .303. It is also statistically significant ($p = .000$).

References

Frankfort-Nachmias, C., & Leon-Guerrero, A. (2006). *Social statistics for a diverse society* (4th ed.). Thousand Oaks, CA: Pine Forge Press.

Frankfort-Nachmias, C., & Leon-Guerrero, A. (2009). *Social statistics for a diverse society* (5th ed.). Thousand Oaks, CA: Pine Forge Press.

7

Correlation and Regression Analysis

R egression analysis allows us to predict one variable from information that we have about other variables. In this chapter, linear regression will be addressed. Linear regression is a type of analysis that is performed on interval ratio variables, although through the use of dummy variables, for instance, it is possible to incorporate data from variables with lower levels of measurement (i.e., nominal and ordinal). First, we will begin with a bivariate regression example and then add some more detail to the analysis.

Bivariate Regression

In the case of bivariate regression, the researcher is interested in predicting the value of the dependent variable, Y, from the information that he or she has about the independent variable, X. We will use the example below, where the respondent's occupational prestige score is predicted from number of years of education. Choose the following menus to begin the bivariate regression analysis:

ANALYZE → REGRESSION → LINEAR . . .

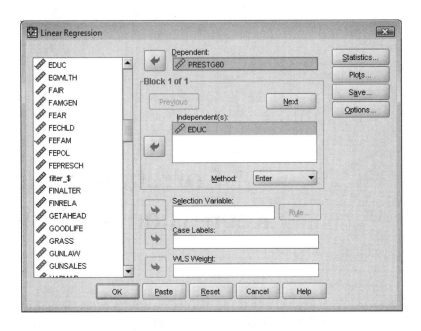

The "Linear Regression" dialog box will appear. Initially, just select the variables of interest and move them into the appropriate slots. Prestg80, respondent's occupational prestige score, should be moved to the "Dependent" slot, and educ, respondent's number of years of education, should be moved to the "Independent" slot. Now, simply click "OK." The following SPSS output will be produced.

Model Summary

Model	R	R Square	Adjusted R Square	Std. Error of the Estimate
1	.522ª	.273	.273	11.941

a. Predictors: (Constant), HIGHEST YEAR OF SCHOOL COMPLETED

In the first column of the model summary, the output will yield Pearson's r, as well as r-square. SPSS also computes an adjusted r-square for those interested in using that value. R-square, like lambda, gamma, and Somers' d, is a PRE statistic that reveals the proportional reduction in error by introducing the dependent variable(s).

ANOVA^a

Model		Sum of Squares	df	Mean Square	F	Sig.
1	Regression	228133.019	1	228133.019	1600.031	.000^b
	Residual	607535.088	4261	142.580		
	Total	835668.107	4262			

a. Dependent Variable: RS OCCUPATIONAL PRESTIGE SCORE (1980)

b. Predictors: (Constant), HIGHEST YEAR OF SCHOOL COMPLETED

Analysis of variance (ANOVA) values are given in the above table of the linear regression output.

Coefficients^a

Model		Unstandardized Coefficients		Standardized Coefficients	t	Sig.
		B	Std. Error	Beta		
1	(Constant)	13.495	.789		17.111	.000
	HIGHEST YEAR OF SCHOOL COMPLETED	2.290	.057	.522	40.000	.000

a. Dependent Variable: RS OCCUPATIONAL PRESTIGE SCORE (1980)

The coefficients table reveals the actual regression coefficients for the regression equation, as well as their statistical significance. In the "Unstandardized Coefficients" column, and in the "B" subcolumn, the coefficients are given. In this case, the "b" value for number of years of education completed is 2.290. The "a" value, or constant, is 13.495. By looking in the last column (Sig.), one can see that both values are statistically significant ($p = .000$). Therefore, we could write the regression model as follows:

$$\hat{Y} = bX + a \quad \hat{Y} = 2.290X^* + 13.495^*$$

*Statistically significant at the $p \le .05$ level.

Correlation

Information about correlation tells us the extent to which variables are related. Below, the Pearson method of computing correlation is requested through SPSS. To examine a basic correlation between two variables, use the following menus:

ANALYZE → CORRELATE → BIVARIATE . . .

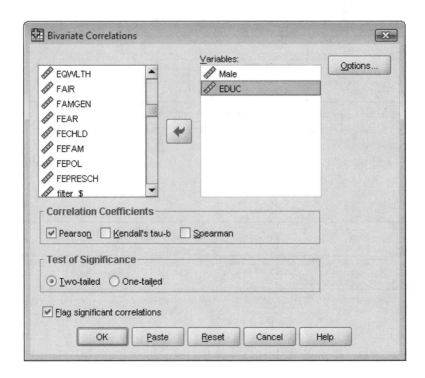

In the "Bivariate Correlations" dialog box, choose the variables that you wish to examine. In the above case, male (dummy variable representing sex; described in further detail below, under "Multiple Regression") and years of education have been selected. The output that results is shown as follows:

Correlations

		Male Dummy Variable	HIGHEST YEAR OF SCHOOL COMPLETED
Male Dummy Variable	Pearson Correlation	1	.015
	Sig. (2-tailed)		.299
	N	4510	4499
HIGHEST YEAR OF SCHOOL COMPLETED	Pearson Correlation	.015	1
	Sig. (2-tailed)	.299	
	N	4499	4499

Note that in the output, the correlation is a very low 0.015, which is not statistically significant (p value is .299).

It is also possible to produce partial correlations. Suppose you are interested in examining the correlation between occupational prestige and education. Further suppose you wish to determine the way that sex affects that correlation. Follow the following menus to produce a partial correlation:

ANALYZE → CORRELATE → PARTIAL . . .

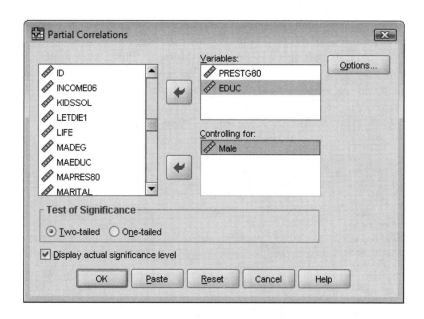

In the "Partial Correlations" dialog box, you will be able to select the variables about which you wish to examine a correlation. You will also be able to select the control variable, around which partial correlations will be computed. In this case, years of education and occupational prestige score have been selected for correlation analysis. The control variable is male. It is possible to include more than one control variable. SPSS produces the following output:

Correlations

Control Variables			RS OCCUPATIONAL PRESTIGE SCORE (1980)	HIGHEST YEAR OF SCHOOL COMPLETED
Male Dummy Variable	RS OCCUPATIONAL PRESTIGE SCORE (1980)	Correlation	1.000	.523
		Significance (2-tailed)	.	.000
		df	0	4260
	HIGHEST YEAR OF SCHOOL COMPLETED	Correlation	.523	1.000
		Significance (2-tailed)	.000	.
		df	4260	0

Here, the correlation is 0.523, and it is statistically significant (p value is .000). Correlation information about variables is useful to have before constructing regression models. Most statistics and research methods books discuss how this information aids in regression analysis.

Multiple Regression

Now, suppose a researcher wished to add an additional independent variable(s) to the analysis. It is very easy to do this using SPSS. All one needs to do is move the additional variables into the "Independent(s)" slot in the regression dialog box, as seen below.

ANALYZE → REGRESSION → LINEAR . . .

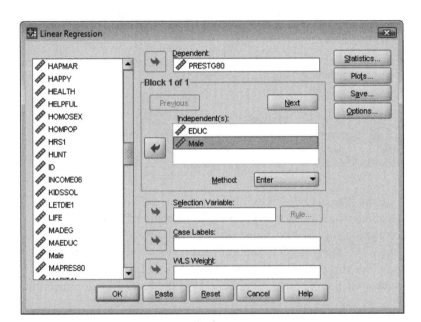

Since linear regression requires interval ratio variables, one must take care when incorporating variables, such as sex, race/ethnicity, religion, and the like. By creating dummy variables from the categories of these nominal variables, you can add this information to the regression equation.

To do this, use the recode function (see Chapter 2: Transforming Variables). Create a dichotomous variable for all but one category, the "omitted" comparison category/attribute, and insert each of those dichotomies into the independent variables slot. The number of dummy variables necessary for a given variable will be equal to $K - 1$, where K is the number of categories of the variable. Dichotomies are an exception to the *cumulative property of levels of measurement,* which tells us that variables measured at higher levels can be treated at lower levels, but *not* vice versa. Dichotomies can be treated as any level of measurement.

For the case of sex, we already have a dichotomy exclusive of transgender and other conditions, so the recode just changes this to one variable: male (alternatively, you could have changed it to "female"). The coding should be binary: 1 for affirmation of the attribute, 0 for respondents not possessing the attribute. Now, as was entered into the previous dialog box, just select the newly recoded variable, male, from the variable bank on the left and move it into the "Independent(s)" slot on the right. You may need to set the variable property to scale in the "Variable View" window so that SPSS will allow that variable to be included in the regression analysis. SPSS Statistics 17.0 tracks variable types and often will not allow you to include variables with a lower level of measurement in analyses requiring variables with higher levels of measurement.

Now, click the "Plots" button, and you will be given the following ("Plots") dialog box:

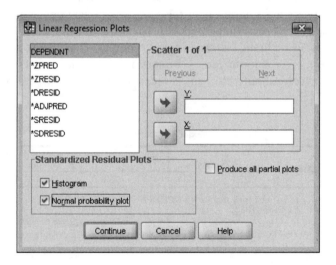

Here, you can avail yourself of a couple of useful graphics: a histogram and a normal probability plot. Click each box to request them. Then click "Continue."

When you are returned to the "Linear Regression" dialog box, now select the "Statistics" button. The following dialog box will appear:

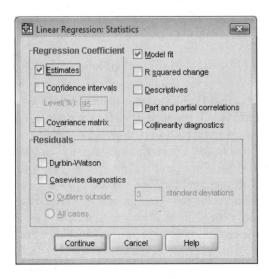

There are a number of options, including descriptive statistics, which you may select to be included in the SPSS linear regression output. Click "Continue" in this box, then click "OK" when returned to the "Linear Regression" dialog box. Below, find tables from the SPSS output. The first two tables give the same sort of information as before in the bivariate regression case: Pearson's *r* (correlation coefficient), *r*-square (PRE), and analysis of variance (ANOVA) values.

Model Summary[a]

Model	R	R Square	Adjusted R Square	Std. Error of the Estimate
1	.523[b]	.273	.273	11.940

a. Dependent Variable: RS OCCUPATIONAL PRESTIGE SCORE (1980)

b. Predictors: (Constant), Male Dummy Variable, HIGHEST YEAR OF SCHOOL COMPLETED

ANOVA[a]

Model		Sum of Squares	df	Mean Square	F	Sig.
1	Regression	228299.106	2	114149.553	800.629	.000[b]
	Residual	607369.001	4260	142.575		
	Total	835668.107	4262			

a. Dependent Variable: RS OCCUPATIONAL PRESTIGE SCORE (1980)

b. Predictors: (Constant), Male Dummy Variable, HIGHEST YEAR OF SCHOOL COMPLETED

The "Coefficients" table again provides the information that can be used to construct the regression model/equation. Note that the dummy variable, male, was not statistically significant.

$$\hat{Y} = bX_1 + bX_2 + a$$

$$\hat{Y} = 2.290X_1^* + 0.397X_2 + 13.316^*$$

*Statistically significant at the $p \le .05$ level.

Coefficients[a]

Model		Unstandardized Coefficients		Standardized Coefficients	t	Sig.
		B	Std. Error	Beta		
1	(Constant)	13.316	.806		16.525	.000
	HIGHEST YEAR OF SCHOOL COMPLETED	2.290	.057	.522	40.000	.000
	Male Dummy Variable	.397	.367	.014	1.079	.281

a. Dependent Variable: RS OCCUPATIONAL PRESTIGE SCORE (1980)

The two graphics that follow show a histogram of the regression standardized residual for the dependent variable as well as the observed by expected cumulative probability for the dependent variable, occupational prestige.

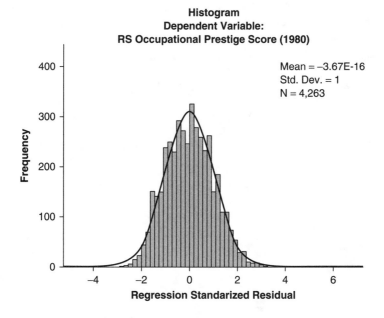

Histogram
Dependent Variable:
RS Occupational Prestige Score (1980)

Mean = −3.67E-16
Std. Dev. = 1
N = 4,263

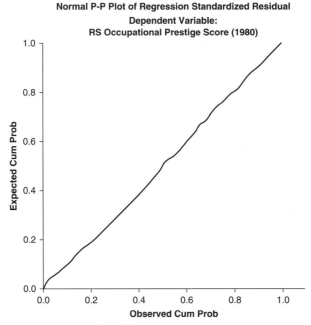

It is possible to add additional variables to the linear regression model you wish to create, like in the dialog box featured below. Interval ratio variables may be included, as well as dummy variables and others such as interaction variables. Interaction variables may be computed using the compute function (in the "transform" menu). More information about computing variables can be found in Chapter 2: Transforming Variables. The computation would consist of variable1*variable2 = interaction variable.

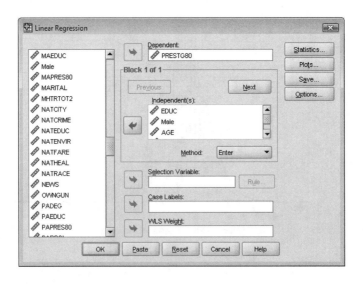

8

Testing Hypotheses Using Means and Cross-Tabulation

S PSS allows for automatic testing of hypotheses without having to make a computation and check a cut point in a table in the back of a statistics book. The actual statistical significance is presented with the results.

Comparing Means

This section explains how to examine differences between two means. Comparing means between groups requires having a variable that will allow for a division into the appropriate groups, in the same way that it is required to split a data file for a comparative analysis.

Suppose you are interested in comparing the occupational prestige scores of respondents and wish to examine the differences between men and women. Select the following menus:

ANALYZE → COMPARE MEANS → MEANS . . .

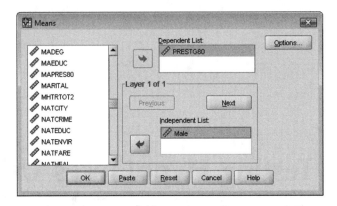

Additional layers can be requested by clicking "Next," then adding the additional variable(s). The DATA → SPLIT FILE option can also be used to compare groups across categories/attributes of a variable. By clicking on the "Options" button, you can customize the cell statistics that SPSS Statistics will report in the output.

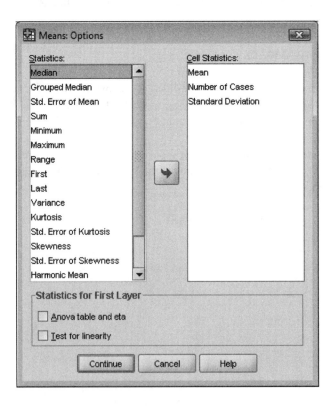

After clicking "Continue" and then "OK" in the "Means" dialog box, SPSS Statistics will generate the following output:

Report

RS OCCUPATIONAL PRESTIGE SCORE (1980)

Male Dummy Variable	Mean	N	Std. Deviation
.00	43.99	2340	13.736
1.00	44.38	1930	14.313
Total	44.17	4270	13.999

A simple table is provided, yielding mean, sample size, and standard deviation for the total sample, as well as each category of the variable of interest, occupational prestige.

Comparing Means: Paired-Samples *t* Test

The paired-samples *t* test can be used when two pieces of information (variables) from the same case are to be compared collectively. An example of such a situation would be a data file containing a group of people who have taken a particular pretest and then an identical posttest after some sort of stimulus had been administered. There are many situations where this method of analysis is appropriate.

From the General Social Survey (GSS) 2006, we can compare parental education by the parents' gender. In other words, we can compare the years of education completed among the respondents' fathers and mothers. To begin, select the following menus:

ANALYZE → COMPARE MEANS → PAIRED SAMPLES T-TEST . . .

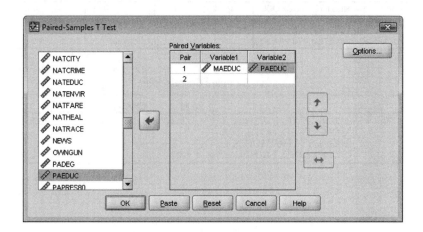

To move a complete entry into the "Paired Variables" box, you will need to select two variables from the variable bank on the left side of the dialog box. Once you have selected two variables and clicked the arrow for each (one right after the other), their names will appear under "Variable1" and "Variable2" for "Pair 1." Additional pairs may be added in subsequent rows.

Should you wish to change the confidence interval (note that the default is 95%) or change the way that missing cases are handled/excluded, click the "Options" button, and you will be given a dialog box to make those selections, as illustrated below.

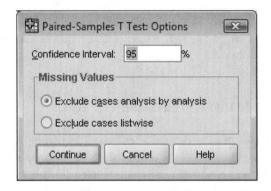

Click "Continue" in the "Options" box, then click "OK" in the "Paired-Samples T-Test" box. What follows is output that SPSS will produce to fulfill your request.

Paired Samples Statistics

		Mean	N	Std. Deviation	Std. Error Mean
Pair 1	HIGHEST YEAR SCHOOL COMPLETED, MOTHER	11.32	2140	4.029	.087
	HIGHEST YEAR SCHOOL COMPLETED, FATHER	11.30	2140	4.531	.098

Paired Samples Correlations

		N	Correlation	Sig.
Pair 1	HIGHEST YEAR SCHOOL COMPLETED, MOTHER & HIGHEST YEAR SCHOOL COMPLETED, FATHER	2140	.700	.000

The above two tables give basic information, such as mean, sample size, standard deviation, standard error, and correlation between the two variables. Note that there is a statistically significant correlation between these two variables.

Paired Samples Test

		Paired Differences							
					95% Confidence Interval of the Difference				
		Mean	Std. Deviation	Std. Error Mean	Lower	Upper	t	df	Sig. (2-tailed)
Pair 1	HIGHEST YEAR SCHOOL COMPLETED, MOTHER - HIGHEST YEAR SCHOOL COMPLETED, FATHER	.016	3.350	.072	-.126	.158	.219	2139	.826

In the third table, the *t* test is performed. Here, *t* = .219. It is not, however, significant at the .05 level or better.

Comparing Means: Independent-Samples *t* Test

Independent-samples *t* tests allow us to compare the mean of a particular variable across independent groups. To look at an example using occupational prestige scale scores, use the following menu selections:

ANALYZE → COMPARE MEANS →
INDEPENDENT-SAMPLES T TEST . . .

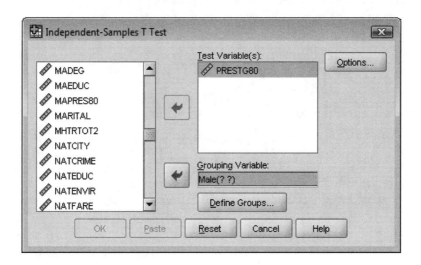

In this dialog box, move the variable of interest, occupational prestige score, into the "Test Variable(s)" box. Next, you will need to select the grouping variable. Male (dummy variable for gender) has been selected. Now, we need to inform SPSS which groups are to be compared. Click the "Define Groups" button.

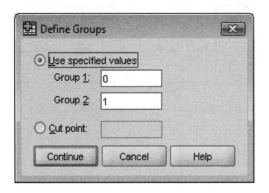

In this "Define Groups" dialog box, fill in the category values for each group. Note that depending on how the grouping variable is categorized, you have the option of selecting a cut point to define the groups. This could be done with age, test scores, and so on.

Click "Continue," which will take you back to the "Independent-Samples T Test" dialog box. You have the option of changing the confidence interval and method of case exclusion. To make those choices, click the "Options" button, and you will be given the dialog box that follows:

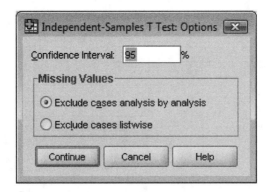

Enter the changes you would like to make, if any, then click "Continue" and then click "OK" in the original dialog box. The output below will be generated by SPSS in response to your query.

Group Statistics

	Male Dummy Variable	N	Mean	Std. Deviation	Std. Error Mean
RS OCCUPATIONAL PRESTIGE SCORE (1980)		2340	43.99	13.736	.284
		1930	44.38	14.313	.326

Independent Samples Test

		Levene's Test for Equality of Variances		t-test for Equality of Means						95% Confidence Interval of the Difference	
		F	Sig.	t	df	Sig. (2-tailed)	Mean Difference	Std. Error Difference		Lower	Upper
RS OCCUPATIONAL PRESTIGE SCORE (1980)	Equal variances assumed	1.760	.185	-.918	4268	.359	-.395	.430		-1.239	.449
	Equal variances not assumed			-.914	4046.839	.361	-.395	.432		-1.242	.452

Basic statistics are given in the first table. The second table reveals the results and significance (or lack thereof in this case) of the t test.

Chi-Square

The chi-square test statistic is used to test statistical independence or goodness of fit. It is used for categorical data. Chi-square summarizes the differences between the observed frequencies (f_o) and the expected frequencies (f_e) in a bivariate table. The observed frequencies are those produced from the raw data. To compute the expected frequencies for any given cell in a bivariate table, multiply the column marginal by the row marginal, then divide by N. The obtained chi-square is then calculated by

$$\chi^2 = \sum \frac{(f_o - f_e)}{f_e}$$

There are two menu selections that will produce chi-square results. The first is demonstrated here. To perform a chi-square analysis, choose the following menu options:

ANALYZE → NONPARAMETRIC TESTS → CHI-SQUARE . . .

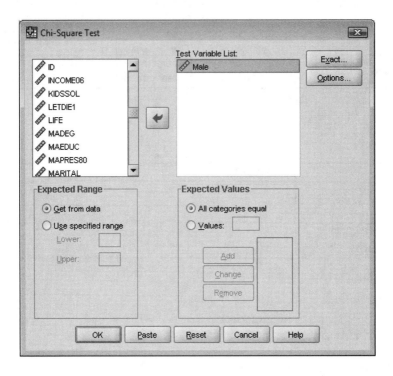

Now, in the "Chi-Square Test" dialog box, choose the variable that you would like to test. In this case, we chose male, the dummy variable representing gender. For expected values, by leaving the button selected for "All categories equal," the expectation is that 50% of the respondents will be men and 50% will be women.

By clicking on the "Options" button, you will be given a dialog box that allows you to request additional information and determine the method by which cases should be excluded.

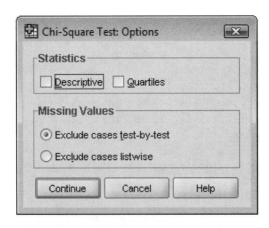

When these decisions have been made, click "Continue," then click "OK" in the "Chi-Square Test" dialog box. The output that follows will be provided by SPSS:

Male Dummy Variable

	Observed N	Expected N	Residual
.00	2507	2255.0	252.0
1.00	2003	2255.0	-252.0
Total	4510		

Test Statistics

	Male Dummy Variable
Chi-Square	56.323[a]
df	1
Asymp. Sig.	.000

a. 0 cells (.0%) have expected frequencies less than 5. The minimum expected cell frequency is 2255.0.

The first table provides the observed and expected amounts and of course the residual or difference. The second table yields the chi-square value and degrees of freedom, and it reveals whether it is statistically significant. In this case, chi-square = 56.323 with 1 degree of freedom (*df*) and is statistically significant.

If you would like to produce full cross-tabulations, such as those detailed in Chapter 6, included with the chi-square information, see the following example by selecting the following menus:

ANALYZE → DESCRIPTIVES → CROSSTABS . . .

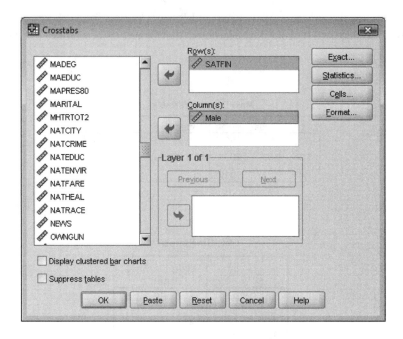

Click the "Statistics" button, and you will be presented with the following dialog box:

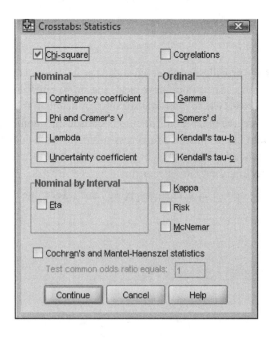

Select the chi-square option, leaving a checkmark in the associated box. Click "Continue," then "OK" back in the "Crosstabs" window. This will produce the following SPSS output.

SATISFACTION WITH FINANCIAL SITUATION * Male Dummy Variable Crosstabulation

Count

		Male Dummy Variable		
		.00	1.00	Total
SATISFACTION WITH FINANCIAL SITUATION	SATISFIED	489	407	896
	MORE OR LESS	741	569	1310
	NOT AT ALL SAT	458	316	774
Total		1688	1292	2980

Chi-Square Tests

	Value	df	Asymp. Sig. (2-sided)
Pearson Chi-Square	3.580[a]	2	.167
Likelihood Ratio	3.585	2	.167
Linear-by-Linear Association	3.550	1	.060
N of Valid Cases	2980		

a. 0 cells (.0%) have expected count less than 5. The minimum expected count is 335.57.

Note that the chi-square value of 3.580 (two degrees of freedom) is not statistically significant according to the results presented in this output.

9

Analysis of Variance

Analysis of variance (ANOVA) is an inferential statistics technique that involves a statistical test for significance of differences between mean scores of at least two groups across one or more than one variable. ANOVA can be used to test for statistical significance using categorical independent variables in conjunction with a continuous dependent variable. ANOVA is based on the comparison of variance between groups to the variance within groups, emerging as the F ratio.

One-Way ANOVA

To perform a one-way ANOVA test, use the following menus:

ANALYZE → COMPARE MEANS → ONE-WAY ANOVA . . .

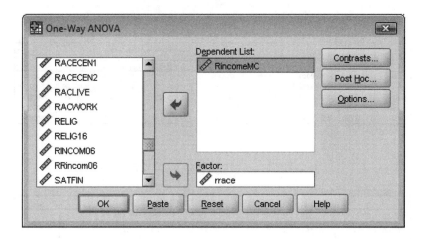

In the dialog box that is presented, choose the dependent and independent (factor) variables for your analysis. Click the "Options" button to customize your selections further. You will be given the following dialog box.

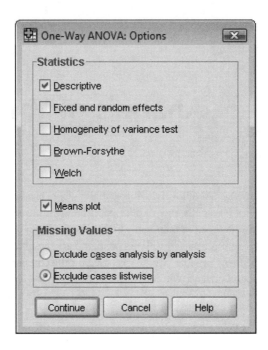

Here, descriptive statistics have been requested, as well as a plot of the means. Cases have been excluded list-wise. The output that follows begins with the descriptive statistic information and is followed next by the ANOVA results.

Descriptives

Respondent's Income Recode

	N	Mean	Std. Deviation	Std. Error	95% Confidence Interval for Mean Lower Bound	Upper Bound	Minimum	Maximum
other	125	40450.0000	38230.18937	3419.41209	33682.0256	47217.9744	500.00	175000.00
white	1906	41690.9759	36176.91554	828.64800	40065.8231	43316.1287	500.00	175000.00
black	358	33030.0279	27694.47986	1463.69874	30151.4723	35908.5836	500.00	175000.00
Hispanic	277	27420.5776	24561.90439	1475.78181	24515.3589	30325.7963	500.00	175000.00
Total	2666	38987.0593	34536.45084	668.87911	37675.4846	40298.6339	500.00	175000.00

ANOVA

Respondent's Income Recode

	Sum of Squares	df	Mean Square	F	Sig.
Between Groups	63964701352.444	3	21321567117.481	18.222	.000
Within Groups	3114757852192.191	2662	1170081837.788		
Total	3178722553544.636	2665			

The means plot has also been provided, as requested.

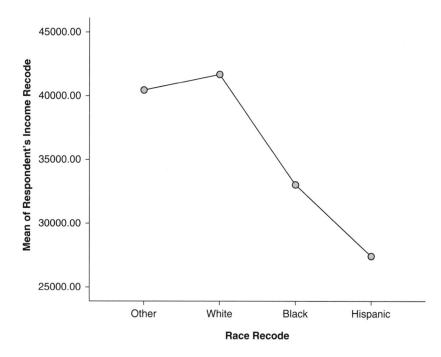

ANOVA With Regression

To examine ANOVA in a regression model, use the following menus:

ANALYZE → REGRESSION → LINEAR . . .

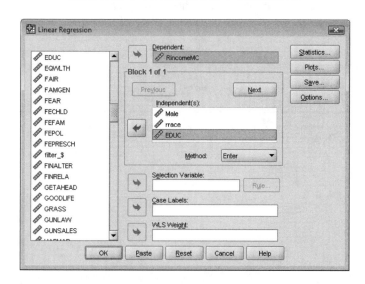

When presented with the "Linear Regression" dialog box, enter your dependent variable and independent variables. To obtain additional partial correlation values or estimates, click the "Statistics" button and mark the appropriate boxes in that dialog box.

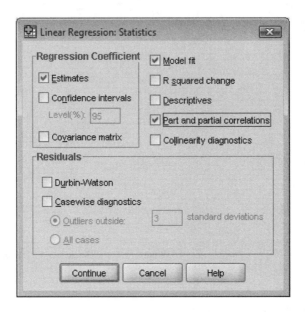

After clicking "Continue" in the above dialog box, then "OK" in the "Linear Regression" dialog box, the following output will be presented. Note the sum of squares and mean squares have been provided, as well as the F statistic and its p value (indicating whether it is statistically significant).

Model Summary

Model	R	R Square	Adjusted R Square	Std. Error of the Estimate
1	.428[a]	.183	.182	31248.91482

a. Predictors: (Constant), HIGHEST YEAR OF SCHOOL COMPLETED, Male Dummy Variable, Race Recode

ANOVA[a]

Model		Sum of Squares	df	Mean Square	F	Sig.
1	Regression	5.816E11	3	1.939E11	198.543	.000[b]
	Residual	2.594E12	2656	9.765E8		
	Total	3.175E12	2659			

a. Dependent Variable: Respondent's Income Recode

b. Predictors: (Constant), HIGHEST YEAR OF SCHOOL COMPLETED, Male Dummy Variable, Race Recode

Coefficients[a]

Model		Unstandardized Coefficients		Standardized Coefficients	t	Sig.	Correlations		
		B	Std. Error	Beta			Zero-order	Partial	Part
1	(Constant)	-19385.715	3413.877		-5.679	.000			
	Male Dummy Variable	17725.217	1213.151	.257	14.611	.000	.243	.273	.256
	Race Recode	-1839.808	880.643	-.038	-2.089	.037	-.132	-.041	-.037
	HIGHEST YEAR OF SCHOOL COMPLETED	3780.962	202.401	.340	18.681	.000	.340	.341	.328

a. Dependent Variable: Respondent's Income Recode

10

Editing Output

The SPSS Output Editor allows a great degree of freedom for editing charts, tables, and other output. This information can all be exported to other computer programs for inclusion in other documents. Most popular, the information and graphics from SPSS Statistics can be suitably imported and handled within Microsoft Word, as well as other computer word-processing programs.

Editing Basic Tables

The first table below was produced by default by SPSS for a "Compare Means" function request, using the following procedure:

ANALYZE → COMPARE MEANS → MEANS . . .

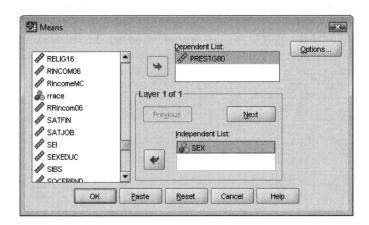

Report

RS OCCUPATIONAL PRESTIGE SCORE (1980)

RESPONDENTS' SEX	Mean	N	Std. Deviation
MALE	44.38	1930	14.313
FEMALE	43.99	2340	13.736
Total	44.17	4270	13.999

The next table has been edited. Labels have been added/edited, and at least one column was resized. You can directly edit the table in the SPSS "Viewer" window by clicking on the table and moving cells, double-clicking and retyping labels, and so on. This is done much the same way that table editing is done using a spreadsheet, such as Microsoft Excel.

Job Prestige by Gender, GSS 2006

RS OCCUPATIONAL PRESTIGE SCORE (1980)

Respondents' Gender	Mean	N	Std. Deviation
MEN	44.38	1930	14.313
WOMEN	43.99	2340	13.736
Total	44.17	4270	13.999

You can also use the SPSS Statistics Pivoting Trays function to change the layout of the table if you wish:

EDIT → EDIT CONTENT → IN VIEWER . . .

You could also elect to edit in a separate window, where all features would be the same. The only difference is that the table itself will pop up in a new window in addition to the "Pivoting Trays" window displayed below.

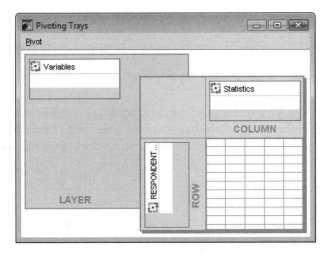

The SPSS Statistics "Pivoting Trays" window gives the user more direct control over the features of the table, including the structure of the variables. This is particularly useful when there are multiple variables in the analysis, including one or more control variables.

Copying to Microsoft Word

There are several options for getting an SPSS table into MS Word. One way is to select the table in the SPSS Output Editor by clicking on it once. Then "copy" the table by choosing the menu:

EDIT → COPY

The keyboard shortcut for that function is <Control> + <C> on a Microsoft Windows PC and <APPLE> + <C> on an Apple Macintosh computer.

At this point, you can "paste" the output into the word processor (e.g., Microsoft Word). This can be done by selecting the following menus in MS Word:

EDIT → PASTE

Again, there is a keyboard shortcut for this function: <Control> + <C> on a PC and <APPLE> + <C> on an Apple Computer.

By copying and pasting in this way, you will still have editing functions over the tables in MS Word. It can, however, be a bit more cumbersome to do the table editing in Word, and it can also pose layout complications. For instance, resizing the table size may necessitate recalibrating font sizes within the table as well as many row and column dimensions. It usually benefits the user to do the table editing in SPSS Statistics and then, when editing is complete, to copy the table object and then select the following menus in Microsoft Word (or similar menus in another word-processing program):

EDIT → PASTE SPECIAL (Then double-click "Picture.")

This will paste the table into Word as a largely noneditable (but resizable) object. While the internal characteristics of the table can no longer be changed at this point, placement and sizing of the table are much easier this way.

Exporting Output

It is possible to have SPSS Statistics automatically export the elements of an output file into separate objects that can be used individually or read into some other program (e.g., a word processor). Another option is to transform the output file in its entirety into another document type for use with another editing/graphics program or word-processing program. Follow the following menus:

FILE → EXPORT . . .

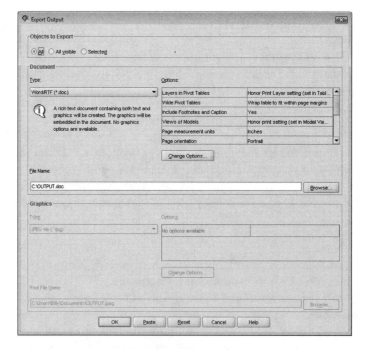

Under "Objects to Export," select what to export: all output, all visible output, or selected output only. Selected output only would include only those

Output Viewer elements that you had clicked to highlight prior to opening the "Export Output" window.

Under "Document," select the format in which you would like the exported files to be saved. Also, you have the option to name the directory where the new files will be saved, under "File Name," if the default location is not satisfactory.

If, under "Document," you select "Graphics only," the lower part of the window under "Graphics" will no longer be dimmed, and you can select the type of graphic file to which SPSS will write your output. You can choose from the list of file types. By selecting JPEG, all of the charts and tables will be saved as separate *.JPG files, which can be imported into other programs and handled like graphic objects.

Editing Charts and Graphs

The SPSS Statistics Output Viewer allows for interactive editing of charts and graphs. Not only can labels, titles, number, legends, and so forth be added and edited, but the very type and style of the chart or graph can be changed from the output interface.

Suppose you create a clustered bar graph, such as the one that is created below:

GRAPHS → CHART BUILDER . . .

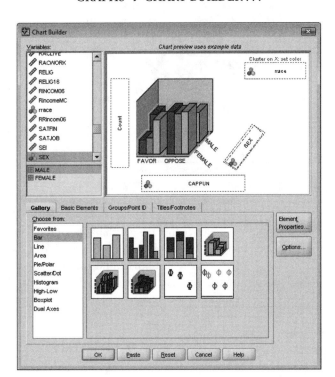

For this graph, we wish to examine the dependent variable, cappun (opinion about capital punishment/the death penalty for murder), as distributed across race/ethnicity and gender. We will use race and sex, respectively, to analyze those dimensions.

Click "OK" to produce the bar graph. Now, for a more comprehensive and interactive way to edit the bar graph (or any other SPSS chart or graph), select and double-click the chart or graph. A new "Chart Editor" window will pop up, as pictured below.

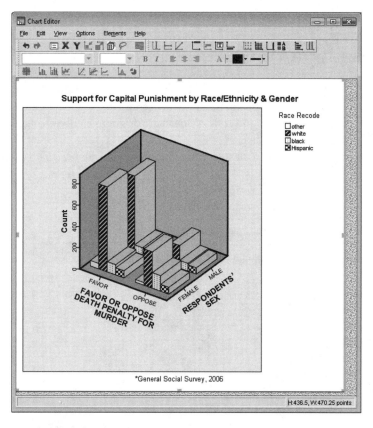

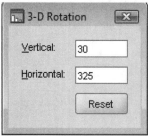

Notice that the graph has been rotated vertically, so that we can better see the bars. You can change the vertical and horizontal rotations on the overall image by using the following menus. For this example, the vertical rotation was augmented to 30 degrees.

EDIT → 3-D ROTATION

A great deal of editing options are available in the "Table Properties" window, which can be accessed by selecting the following menus (or shortcut).

EDIT → PROPERTIES (or selecting <CONTROL> + <T>)

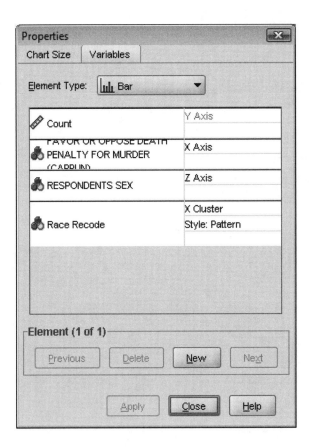

By selecting "element" type, you can change the type of graph, from a bar graph to some other type of graph, such as a pie chart or an area graph. It is not necessary to go through and rerun the graph/chart function. It can be rebuilt directly from this editor window.

By selecting "Style" by the X Cluster variable, "Sex," you can choose whether to have the graph in color, black and white patterns, or some other method of illustration. For this example, the "pattern" style was chosen over the color option, as is often best decided when the printing options are monochrome, such as a monochrome laser printer.

11

Advanced Applications

Merging Data From Multiple Files

There are typically two ways a user wants to merge files. One way is to combine two data files that contain the same variables but consist of different cases (e.g., two or more waves of surveys completed by different people but including the same information). Another way is to have additional variables to add to existing cases (e.g., second round of responses from the same respondents). Note that you must be doing this from the "Data Editor" window containing the file (active data set) to which you wish to add cases or variables.

First, suppose you want to add cases:

DATA → MERGE FILES → ADD CASES . . .

If you have already opened the data file in another SPSS "Data Editor" window, then you can select "An open dataset" and choose from the list. Otherwise, select "An external SPSS data file" and locate the file you wish to add. Both files, of course, need to be in SPSS (*.sav) format. If the file you are adding is not in SPSS data format, then you should first import that file into SPSS before carrying out the merge function. You will be presented with a new dialog box, such as the one that follows:

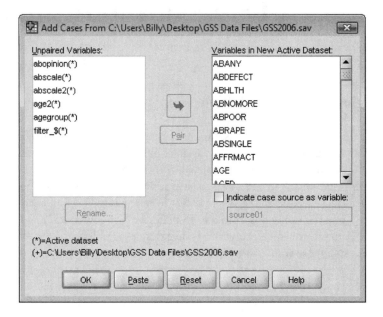

Assuming there are no unpaired variables or you are not concerned with pairing variables (same variables in two different data sets, each with a different name), select "OK," and SPSS will perform the addition of cases to your data file.

Now, suppose you want to add variables:

FILE → DATA → ADD VARIABLES . . .

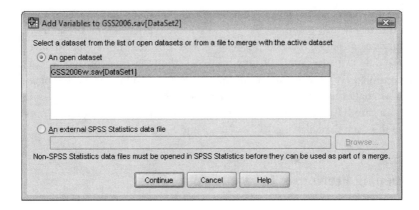

Again, select the appropriate file, whether it is open in another instance (window) of SPSS or located on a disk or server connected to your computer. Click "Continue," and you will be presented with the next dialog box.

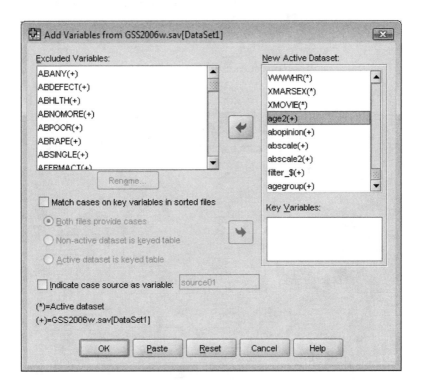

The "New Active Dataset" box shows the variables that will be contained in the newly merged data file. The excluded variables are those that are duplicates in name. If any of those are not duplicates but happen to have the same name, then select each one and click the "Rename" button to correct the problem. If you are not certain that the cases are in identical order between the two data files, then you must match the cases by some identifying variable (e.g., a case ID); select the variable that contains that information and move it into the "Key Variables" box. Click "OK," and SPSS will perform the merge.

Opening Previously Created Syntax Files

Syntax files provide computer code to instruct SPSS to perform functions. Most of these functions can be achieved by using the "point-and-click" method that this book uses. That is, functions can be performed by using the menus at the top of the "Data Editor" window. Creating syntax code using SPSS syntax computer language is not addressed in this book. If you have an SPSS syntax file, however, with code for performing SPSS tasks, open it as follows:

FILE → OPEN → SYNTAX

You will get a dialog box such as the one below:

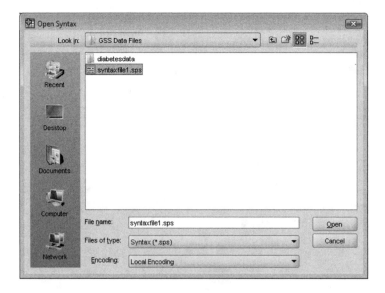

Navigate your computer files, locate your file, and open it. The syntax code will appear in a "Syntax Editor" window, such as the one that follows. Select the portion of the code that you wish to run. (The example below runs frequency information on a data file that is supposed to already be opened.) Click the "Run" button to execute the computer code. (The "Run" button is the blue triangle.) You can also type <CTRL> + <R> or select the following from the menu:

RUN → SELECTION

From the menu, you also have the option to run all or from a particular point to the end. The menu option also affords the option to choose which lines (from, to) of syntax code to run.

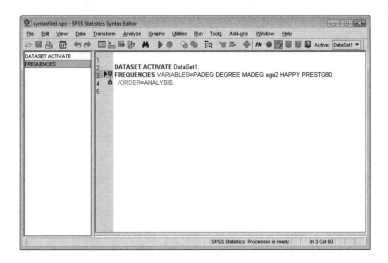

Creating New SPSS Syntax Files

While this book will not provide detailed information about creating syntax files, there are a few things about syntax files that may be useful, even for those users who have no intention of writing code to perform SPSS functions. To create the new syntax file, select the following menu options:

FILE → NEW → SYNTAX

A new window, "Syntax Editor," will appear. Whatever information is typed into this interface will comprise the syntax file. All or part of what is typed into this interface can be used at a later time or immediately.

With any of the SPSS "point-and-click" functions, those operations imple-mented using the menus at the top of the editor windows, there is an option to select "Paste" instead of clicking "OK." What this does is to not execute the function(s) but instead record the instructions for performing the functions in a syntax window. A user may choose to save the instructions for use later or run them immediately and save a copy for future use or reference. What is pasted are the instructions that SPSS gives "behind the scenes" for that particular function (e.g., frequency distributions).

Saving pasted SPSS syntax files can be useful for those who are performing many operations that are repetitive or similar across variables, particularly if they are more complicated functions. Saving syntax files also provides a complete record of how a data file was altered, which can be helpful to some users since SPSS will show the altered data file only and not provide a list of updates that have been made.

About the Author

William E. Wagner, III, PhD, is Associate Professor of Sociology at California State University (CSU), Channel Islands. Prior to coming to CSU, Channel Islands, he served as a member of the faculty and Director of the Institute for Social and Community Research at CSUB. His MA and PhD degrees (sociology) are from the University of Illinois, Chicago. His BA degree (mathematics) is from St. Mary's College of Maryland. He has published in national and regional scholarly journals on topics such as urban sociology, sports, homophobia, and academic status.